OF MANY
COLORS

*"One day somebody
should remind us
that, even though
there may be political
and ideological dif-
ferences between us,
the Vietnamese are
our brothers, the
Russians are our bro-
thers, the Chinese are
our brothers; and one
day, we've got to sit
down together at the
table of brotherhood."*
*—Martin Luther
King Jr., 1967*

UNIVERSITY OF MASSACHUSETTS PRESS · *Amherst*

OF MANY COLORS

Portraits

of

Multiracial

Families

Photos by Gigi Kaeser · Interviews by Peggy Gillespie

Introduction by Glenda Valentine

Publication of this book has been made
possible by a generous donation from
the Tsunami Foundation

Based on the exhibit *Of Many Colors,*
text © 1994 by Peggy Gillespie;
photographs © 1994 by Gigi Kaeser
Text © 1997 by Peggy Gillespie
Photographs © 1997 by Gigi Kaeser
Designed by Mary Mendell
Photographs printed by Geoffrey Bluh
Typeset in Adobe Berkeley
Printed and bound in Singapore
Library of Congress Cataloging-in-
Publication Data
Kaeser, Gigi.
Of many colors : portraits of multiracial
families / photos by Gigi Kaeser; interviews
by Peggy Gillespie.
p.   cm.
Includes bibliographical references (p.   ).
ISBN 1-55849-100-7 (cloth : alk. paper).—
ISBN 1-55849-101-5 (pbk. : alk. paper)
1. Interracial marriage—United States—
Interviews. 2. Interracial marriage—United
States—Portraits. 3. Children of interracial
marriage—United States. 4. Interracial adop-
tion—United States. 5. Family—United States.
6. Ethnicity—United States. I. Gillespie,
Peggy, 1948–. II. Title.   HQ1031.K33   1997
306.84'6—dc21   97-6530 CIP
British Library Cataloguing in Publication
 data are available.

To Greg Gillespie for his support on every level, and to our daughter Jay who teaches everyone she meets to look beyond stereotypes.

—Peggy Gillespie

To Michael

—Gigi Kaeser

And to all the multiracial families in this book who have courageously opened their private lives to the public eye, we thank you.

—Peggy Gillespie and Gigi Kaeser

CONTENTS

PREFACE

My husband and I are both white and our nine-year-old daughter's racial heritage is African American, Native American, and Caucasian. Her friends include many children of color who also have been adopted by white parents, as well as many children whose parents are in interracial relationships.

To investigate some of the issues faced by families like ours, I teamed up with Gigi Kaeser and set out to find multiracial families who would be willing to be photographed and interviewed for an exhibit. We did not have to look far. Within driving distance of our homes in western Massachusetts, we were able to locate thirty-five families who agreed to participate. Later we added several more from other areas of the United States. Although this sample is not meant to be comprehensive, it does include a fairly wide range of situations and viewpoints. To produce the text, I interviewed each family at length and then edited the transcript into brief excerpts from each family member. I invited the participants to review and modify their own quotations to reflect as clearly as possible their personal perspectives. Without exception, everyone responded to my questions with great candor and passion.

When we completed the interviews and photography sessions, Gigi and I called the exhibit: "√ OTHER: Portraits of Multiracial Families," because many members of these families must check the racial category "Other" on official forms. Multiple copies of the exhibit (now entitled "Of Many Colors") have been criss-crossing the nation, traveling to public and private schools, universities, museums, libraries, and houses of worship. Over and over, people have told us how moved they were by seeing the exhibit. Many said they wished to have something tangible to take home with them. They wanted to read the words and see the faces of these families again. For that reason, we decided to create this book.

Peggy Gillespie

This collection of photographs originally had some pictures in color and some in black and white. As soon as we began talking to and photographing these families, we saw that black and white and color—the words and the ideas—were the terms of our project. I thought of how the words that I had been taught to use had changed: colored, Negro, black, Afro-American, African American, person of color. These words changed as attitudes changed, as the people themselves got more control of what they were called. The words lost, then regained, their coloration. And I believe that a black-and-white photograph is the most real and has the most color.

As I hectored each family into being natural for the camera, they all were patient and good-humored. I want to thank them for that and for everything they taught me while we worked on this project.

Gigi Kaeser

INTRODUCTION

Glenda Valentine

When Richard Loving brought his new bride home to his native state of Virginia in 1958, he received a rude welcome. Because Loving, a white man, had married Mildred Jeter, a black woman, he was arrested for violating the state's antimiscegenation laws. For his crime, Loving could have been sentenced to five years in prison. Instead, he received a suspended sentence with the condition that he and his wife leave Virginia and not return for a period of twenty-five years.

Feeling they had done nothing wrong, the Lovings sued the state. Their case, *Loving v. Commonwealth of Virginia*, became a nine-year legal battle that ended in the U.S. Supreme Court in 1967. The Court's decision declared unconstitutional all laws against intermarriage—in Virginia and fifteen other states.

The family portraits in this book are proof that interracial marriage is more socially acceptable today than it was in 1958. Although statistics on the current number of interracial marriages in America vary, an educated guess can be made. According to the U.S. Census Bureau, in 1992 there were approximately 246,000 black-white married couples. Demographers estimate that black-white unions constitute about 20 percent of all interracial marriages, therefore we can estimate that there are well over one million interracial married couples in America today. This increase has yet to equal acceptance.

While the number of mixed-race families in America is steadily rising, interracial marriage remains a controversial issue that too often strains friendships and divides families. Many of the families in this book can and do testify to this fact.

What is it about the mixing of races that bothers some people so? It seems the most divisive issue is not that two adults of different racial backgrounds choose to join their lives in matrimony, but that these adults will produce mixed-race children. Children who are born into the great chasm of America's racial divide. Children who defy traditional racial categorization and, in doing so, become threats to—and victims of—America's entire concept of race and the social order that has been built upon it.

Throughout history, America has depended on very clear racial categories for its social, political, economic, and psychological organization. The country's first census, in 1790, divided the population into four groups: free white males, free white females, slaves, and other persons (including free blacks and Indians). By the early nineteenth century, the census specified that slaves were to be identified with a "B" if they were black and an "M" if they were mulatto.

In 1815, Thomas Jefferson tried to nail down the science of racial categorization. He devised an intricate algebraic equation to show that "one-fourth Negro blood, mixed with any portion of white, constitutes the mulatto."

To guarantee that mixed-race children of slaveholders would be included in the slave population, the law of hypodescent, better known as the "one-drop" rule, was promoted in the antebellum South. The one-drop rule evolved out of the premise that each race had its own blood type and that a single drop of "Negro blood" was sufficient to define a person as black. It was, scientifically speaking, nonsense—but it relieved the slaveholders of having to recognize that many of their enslaved progeny were essentially white. Today it is estimated that between 75 and 95 percent of blacks could define themselves as something other than black because of their mixed heritage.

As many of the stories in this book illustrate, the one-drop rule endures to some extent today. Many people of black and white ancestry encounter more acceptance in the black community and therefore define themselves as black. But these stories also demonstrate how the one-drop rule is slowly being eliminated by individuals of mixed heritage who are no longer willing to adhere to it. They are determined to acknowledge the diversity of their heritage and they refuse to limit their identity to one race or another. They choose not to confine themselves to traditional racial categories. They are asking for the addition of a "multiracial" category on census forms and other documents.

Of course, there are people who are uncomfortable with the notion of a multiracial category and question its value. They ask: "Wouldn't a new category be a continuation of the divisions that have plagued us for so long?" "How would such a category affect the government's ability to fight racial discrimination?" "Wouldn't a multiracial category become a comical extension of the one-drop rule—nearly everyone could say: 'I've got one drop of something—I must be multiracial!'?" The latter is closer to truth than absurdity since anthropologists tell us that we *are* nearly all multiracial.

Perhaps a multiracial category would help blur the boundaries between groups and bring us a small step toward eliminating the deeply embedded, pseudoscientific construct of race that divides our society. As one college professor explained, the addition of a multiracial category "has the potential for undermining the very basis of racism, which is its categories."

The debate over racial categories is bewildering because, like the debate over transracial adoption, it is based on ever-changing social standards rather than scientific evidence. Many people believe that children in transracial adoptions—especially black or biracial children adopted by white families—are more prone to difficulties with development of personal and racial identity. However, studies have failed to demonstrate significantly this theory. A 1994 study by Adoptive Families of America found that by four different measures of psychological health—identity, self-esteem, adoption identity, and attachment—transracially adopted youth fare as well as their white counterparts in same-race adoptions.

The debate over transracial adoption became public during the 1960s and '70s, when the pool of healthy white babies available for adoption began to shrink and more babies of color were placed with white families. Something else was happening in America during this time. The black identity or black power movement was engulfing the nation. With such an extreme focus on black identity, transracial adoptions involving black and mixed-race children were more closely scrutinized, and many white families were accused of failing to nurture the black heritage of their adopted children. The National Association of Black Social Workers (NABSW) asserted that only black families could effectively provide black children with a positive sense of racial identity. In 1972, the NABSW issued a resolution opposing the adoption of black and biracial children by white families. By 1987, thirty-five states had laws prohibiting the adoption of black children by white families, and in 1989, the NABSW reaffirmed its opposition to transracial adoptions.

Throughout the years, the NABSW's policy met with great criticism, the most significant of which came in the form of legislative action. In August 1996, as approximately fifty thousand black and biracial children remained trapped in America's foster care system, President Bill Clinton signed a bill making it illegal to prohibit adoptions based on race. The Reverend Jesse Jackson called the bill a reaffirmation of the Civil Rights Act, saying, "transracial adoption, like intermarriage, must be protected by law and must be open as an option for everyone."

Just as every photograph is better appreciated when surrounded by a complementary frame, the brief historical information on interracial marriage and transracial adoption presented here is meant to frame each of the following family portraits. When viewed in this historical context, the images, experiences, and insights of each family have more impact and provide a clearer picture of how mixed-race families are contradicting stereotypes, challenging racism, and demonstrating that people of different races can live together. The families in this book are truly diverse, with members from black, white, Asian, Latino, Native American, and other ethnic backgrounds.

These families—whether by marriage or adoption—have made a commitment to love and cherish each other in spite of society's disdain. Like Richard Loving and Mildred Jeter thirty years ago, the families you are about to meet have courageously chosen to bridge the racial divide. May their portraits be symbols of hope for all of us.

FAMILY

PORTRAITS

*"When one is in love,
a cliff becomes a
meadow."*
—*Ethiopian Saying*

THE AKAMATSU/GATSIK FAMILY

Norma Akamatsu · Ron Gatsik · Haru Akamatsu · Sarah (8)

NORMA

I always thought "Norma" was an odd name for a little Japanese American girl, but my mother had chosen my name for a very special reason. When my mother was growing up in California, during the pre–World War II era, it was a period of racial discrimination against Asians. The first white girl to befriend my mother in high school was named "Norma," so she named me after that girl. Knowing that story, I took two meanings from my name. First, I saw it as a reminder and a warning that the experience of discrimination and prejudice is a part of my heritage. Secondly, it helped me recognize that people can—as Norma did—transcend those divisions and limitations.

When I was young, my mother hoped I would marry a Japanese American Protestant boy. When I was in my twenties, she hoped I would marry somebody Protestant. By my thirties, she just hoped I would get married to someone nice. By the time I married Ron—a Jewish American—she was happy about it. She was delighted when we gave birth to Sarah.

My mother was born in America, but my father came here when he was eighteen. I grew up with both my parents speaking Japanese, but I think that my Japanese heritage would really be lost to Sarah without my mother living so close to us. Haru makes the Japanese culture real to Sarah.

We were all traveling in Florida, and Sarah was observing black and white people in a department store. She asked me if black people didn't like white people. I said, "Well, there's been a history," and I launched into this whole speech about discrimination. I told Sarah that she, too, is a person of color, and that Grandma Haru was discriminated against when she was a girl because she was Japanese and that she had lived in detention camps during World War II. Then Ron talked about discrimination against the Jews, and he explained that you can be white and be discriminated against, too. Not long after that, Sarah's

"If the earth is going to continue to be a viable habitat for human beings, we're going to have to evolve from 'ethnic cleansing' to the sharing of ethnic information in an open and respectful manner, and perhaps ultimately to an acceptance of 'ethnic blending.'"
—Ron Gatsik

class at school was talking about Martin Luther King Jr. The teacher was surprised that Sarah publicly condemned racism during the discussion. I was glad to hear that she had such strong feelings, and that she wasn't afraid to say them. I would hope that Sarah's biracial and bicultural background would help her to be aware of the dangers of prejudice, and to see that they can be overcome.

RON

I grew up Jewish in a suburban community with a large mixture of black, Jewish, and other ethnic populations. But it wasn't until I went off to college and really got to know people from different places, backgrounds, and cultures that I began to change. I think the Civil Rights movement, the war in Vietnam, and the political work I was doing opened me up to the possibility of marrying outside of Judaism. Having fallen "head over heels" in love with Norma was also a way of saying, "The world needs to change, and I need to change."

When I brought Norma home, my parents (I later learned) were politely and privately quite upset, at least as much because she wasn't Jewish as because she wasn't white. It wasn't until they got to know her as a person and eventually as a mother to Sarah that they made peace with the idea.

We go to Haru's, eat Japanese food, see all of Haru's Japanese "tchachtkes," hear her talk about the Japanese American community in New York City (as a minister's wife, she was the chief social worker, lay therapist, and matriarch of that community for thirty years), and Sarah absorbs that part of her heritage.

Norma and I celebrate Hanukkah and Christmas, and meditate from time to time in the Tibetan Buddhist and Indian spiritual traditions. We think it's important that Sarah realizes that she's an amalgam. Norma and I use the word "Jewpanese" to describe our family. I think our daughter Sarah believes it's a real word.

Last year, Sarah went to school dressed in her kimono. Haru went with Sarah and showed pictures of Japan and talked about Japanese culture to the class. After that, Sarah's school friends seemed to notice that Sarah was a different race. But as near as we can tell, it's never been a problem for her.

The "yang" of Jewish culture and the "yin" of Japanese culture make for an interesting synthesis that has been a dynamic factor in my relationship with Norma for over twenty years. And Sarah clearly manifests both aspects of these culturally determined tendencies.

Multiracial families need to learn how to negotiate the impact of cultural differences. The legacy of racial prejudice and stereotyping resides in each of us and our "unconscious racism" is perhaps most problematic.

If the earth is going to continue to be a viable habitat for human beings, we're going to have to evolve from "ethnic cleansing" to the sharing of ethnic information in an open and respectful manner, and perhaps ultimately to an acceptance of "ethnic blending."

HARU

I was raised in an interfaith household by grandparents and a father who were Shinto, Zen Buddhist, and Buddhist, and my mother had converted to Christianity. Both of my children have married Jewish spouses. These enriching experiences have enabled me to love, accept, and appreciate individuals in all their diversity.

SARAH

My name is Sarah. I am half Japanese and half Jewish. I am what is called biracial.

Once a girl teased me by saying, "We don't want to play with you because you have dark skin." I was pretty upset, but not too upset. I told my mother. She said she would call the girl's mother and tell her what happened, but she wanted time to think about how to do that in the best way since she didn't know the girl's family very well.

To my mother's surprise, the girl came to our house the next day when I was already at school, and she apologized for what she had said to me. My mom thanked her very much. When I came home from school, my mom told me that an amazing thing had happened—that the girl had come over to apologize. "I wonder why she decided to do that," my mom said to me. "I know why," I said. So I told my mom how I had gone to the girl's house on my own, and told her mother about what had happened. And the girl's mother promised to have a talk with her daughter. My mom was very proud of me for having the courage to stand up for myself.

THE AWAD FAMILY

Anne Awad · Omar Awad · Yusef (21) · Asha (14)

ANNE

I was expecting difficulty from my family about Omar—a black man from Somalia—but when I told my mother that I was going to elope with him, she said, "Come home and get married, and we'll gather the family around." I sometimes think that my parents accepted Omar because they saw him as "exotic." They were always saying things to the relatives like, "Omar had servants as a child."

We've struggled to help our children with identity issues. As they build their own lives outside our family, this society will see our children as black people. They need a strong and healthy feeling that they are black by virtue of being biracial. In fact, we've avoided using the term "biracial." We agree that our children are biracial, but we resist that word as the only correct term to define them. We have known people who insist loudly that their children are not black, that they are biracial. Is this a denial of their blackness?

One of our white neighbors has gotten so used to Omar, he has sort of washed Omar's color away. Recently, he told Omar, "Watch out, you need to lock your doors. A black family moved in nearby."

Omar and I have been married for twenty-six years—our multiculturalism has been both a pro and a con for us. The con is that it can be lonely to be different. There aren't many other models of Somali–New Englander marriages. The pro, for me—a white woman in this society—is that I took a risk as a young person, and it has forced me to stay flexible and creative in order to respond to the challenges presented by this society to my family. Had I stayed within white society, I probably would have settled into traditional, judgmental, and confining ways. So I have been saved from that fate!

"I guess it's really special to be two different things. I don't even really think about my parents as two different races—and I don't really think of myself as being in between two different people."
—Asha Awad

7

OMAR

People have driven by when I was out in the garden weeding the beans and screamed racist hate words at me. It really jars you in that place of beauty. Once, I was in the garage with this open window. All of a sudden I heard this whoosh across my scalp. Someone had aimed and fired a high-powered rifle at me. That was fifteen years ago and, only recently, we replaced the pane of glass. I guess I wanted to be reminded of it all those years.

I talk to local "rednecks" and it's amazing that when we discuss things we all know about like tomatoes, I think it makes us able to communicate. I often talked to this one guy about vegetables, and after a while, we talked about the problems of Somalia. He seemed to understand. When you talk to people, walls break down. Now these old farmers send everybody to my chemical laboratory to test their water. How do they relate to other black people? I don't know.

While Anne and I appear to be very different, once we married, we fortunately discovered that we were more alike than different. We share similar personal and ethical values that have stayed with us throughout our life together.

YUSEF

It's interesting being unique. It's good. I'm glad about who I am and how I am. It's hard to express in words.

Asha and I can identify with white people and with black people. There are also Indian and Arabic and Latino people who look very much like us. We can identify with all people.

I try to see beyond the "American culture," so pervasive in the media, to all the diverse ways to see and live life.

ASHA

I guess it's really special to be two different things. I don't even really think about my parents as two different races—and I don't really think of myself as being in between two different people. I guess I'm always going to be seen as being part of a different culture through white people's eyes, but I don't think of myself as different.

THE BARTHOLET FAMILY

Elizabeth Bartholet · Christopher (9) · Michael (7)

ELIZABETH

I have an older biological son, Derek, and I adopted Christopher and Michael as a single parent. My children by adoption are as much inside my skin as any born to me could be. It feels entirely right that they should be here.

Adoption agencies segregate children waiting for homes and prospective parents on the basis of race, with the goal of promoting same-race matches and preventing transracial placements. Black children are, as a result, condemned in large numbers to "foster home limbo," their lives put on hold while they wait for months, years, and often their entire childhoods for color-matched families.

The existence of families in which blacks and whites live in a state of mutual love and commitment, and struggle in this context to understand issues of racial and cultural difference, seems a positive good to be celebrated. The government should not be in the position of discouraging the creation of such families.

As a parent, I revel in the brown skin and thick black hair and dark eyes and Peruvian features that I could not have produced. I have also felt the shock of seeing myself—my intensity, my gestures, my expressions—as I watch these children.

I am enchanted by the tempestuous moods of one child and the laid-back good nature of the other. I am intrigued by the mystery of who they are and will be, and what part I will play in this. I am aware of myriad ways in which my life has been enhanced by these adoptions, and I think of people who have known only biologic parenting as people who are missing a special experience.

I have found myself thinking a lot about some of our assumptions regarding difference. A friend asked me when I first returned to this country with Christopher if his baby babble sounded the same as my birth child Derek's baby babble. It did sound the same, of course, but I had to confess that this was somehow surprising to me, and that on some level I must actually have expected that the

"As a parent, I revel in the brown skin and thick black hair and dark eyes and Peruvian features that I could not have produced."
—Elizabeth Bartholet

four-month-old gurgles would have a particularly Peruvian ring to them.

Last month we celebrated the Inti Raymi, the Incan Sun Festival, with forty Peruvian adoptive families. It featured a Peruvian band and home-cooked Peruvian food. We sang songs about a kind of love that knows no colors and no borders, and we raised money for a poor shantytown near Lima. We recited the words from an Incan prophecy: "When the eagle of the North flies with the condor of the South, the spirit of the land she will awaken." I wondered what people in Peru would think to see this group of North Americans with their Peruvian-born children dancing and singing on the top of a hill in Massachusetts, paying tribute to the Incan god of creation.

Christopher's teacher showed me a picture he had drawn of himself the day before. The children were supposed to use only pencil for this picture, but he had insisted on adding some color. He needed to make his face brown and his rollerblades neon orange and green. I don't know exactly how my boys will identify themselves, who they will be, or where they will seem to belong in the future. My hope is that they will experience a rich sense of choice and connection.

THE BENJAMIN / ZELLERS FAMILY

Sheila Benjamin · Bonnie Zellers · Eric DeMarco Benjamin (18)
Elan Biko Benjamin (1 1/2)

SHEILA

I was raised as the daughter of a career military officer and a homemaker. We lived in military housing areas where there wasn't any separation of races. As a result, I became very comfortable with diversity. Maybe that's why I have no trouble seeing people for who they really are, when many other people can't seem to see past skin color.

Bonnie and I have been together since March 1990. We started out as coworkers, investigating child abuse cases in the state of Maryland, then became friends, and then became lovers and partners in life. My son Marc was fourteen at the time Bonnie and I got together.

Bonnie and I began talking about having children together very early in our relationship because I knew right away that I wanted Bonnie to be the other mother of my children. I saw that she was sweet and kind and tender, and I knew that was what I wanted to bring into my family. I was so right.

Marc had always wanted a sibling, so he was as happy as we were when Bonnie tested positive for pregnancy on Martin Luther King Jr.'s birthday in 1993.

Elan's birth the following September was the most intense and amazing experience. I love the family we have become together and hope for the blessing of more children as we journey through life together.

The hardest part for me now is that the area we live in is not as culturally diverse as we had hoped. We do have a small circle of friends here; mostly white lesbians with children who are supportive of one another. We have great times together but I feel at times that I have to work hard to fit in.

I remember the black community that enveloped me as a child. There were usually groups of three or four other families who took turns going to each others' houses where we would laugh and tease each other in a warm and loving

"I think it's cool that one of my moms is black and my other mom is white. There's no room for racism in our family. That's how it should be."
—Eric DeMarco Benjamin

11

way. Everyone was at ease and felt somehow whole. There was such a warmth and closeness, a way of connecting that we didn't have anywhere else. We came together like the petals of a rosebud. Our body language, our laughter, our talk, our energy was delicious. We all belonged there. We were safe. I resent that there are no oases today that are large enough to hold a family like ours. How incredibly sad that we need safe havens at all.

My oldest son, Marc, had black community when he was growing up with extended family all around him. Now he has quite a multicultural circle of friends.

Being black is something I'm very proud of. It is integral to my identity. I wanted our children to be biracial so that I could share my culture in all its richness and beauty with them. Also, I never wanted to have my connection to my sons questioned, especially in the event that something should happen, God forbid, to Bonnie. Of course, we strongly considered the impact that race would have on Elan's life before making the choice to use a black sperm donor. We wouldn't have made that choice if we didn't believe it would benefit him.

Our hope is that having a multicultural family will provide our children with a fuller picture of what is possible and will open doors for them. Having access to more opportunities and more tools might make it possible for them to become the people they are meant to be.

Of course we have concerns too. We're aware that some biracial teens become very angry with one parent or another as they struggle with their own identities. We were also concerned that Elan would feel alienated from both the black and the white circles, or that he would feel the need to deny part of himself to feel accepted. This isn't a struggle that Bonnie or I have had to fight. However, there are common grounds that we can navigate together. My hope is that we are bonded enough, patient enough, and clear enough to work through all of that together. So far, Elan is very self-confident and grounded in his entire heritage. He is being taught to take pride in himself and bask in the glory of his histories. So, we're hopeful.

In our family we have a deep commitment to justice, to honesty, and to celebrating diversity. Love transcends all would-be barriers between us.

BONNIE

I think everything from the past leads us to where we are in the present. My father was a pastor and my mother was a teacher. I was indoctrinated with all the basic Christian ideology and traditional "family values." Somehow that did lay a foundational belief that all persons have equal worth and beauty.

In my rebellious adolescence, I was angry a lot of the time about how hatefully and fearfully people have learned to treat each other. Ultimately, I learned to let my heart and my "inner knowing" of people lead me into relationships rather than holding onto a culturally proscribed image of who my partner should be. I'm glad my heart led me to Sheila.

Our relationship has always been quite loving and strong, but not always easy. The filters through which we see the world are different; in part this is because we are treated so differently in this society. But, I believe that Sheila and I respect those differences and have learned to broaden our scopes. Some of our differences, such as having different holiday traditions, have given us the chance to sift through all that we carried into this relationship. We've kept what is meaningful to each of us and have created new traditions together as a family.

As a lesbian couple, there are few external supports, and as an interracial couple, there is a whole power system operating around us that seeks to throw us off balance at any given time. So I think we're doing an amazing job working things through together.

Maybe we're stronger because we've had to build a united front; or maybe it's because we're such good friends; or maybe it's because Sheila has such a good sense of humor and has taught me how to relax and enjoy.

Parenting puts into practice all that we believe about ourselves and our place in the world. We want so much for our sons to be truly proud of who they are, to walk tall and use their full voices. We know that there are many forces against them. There are people who are ready to question or ridicule or deny them because of their race or their family. People are afraid of young black men and people are afraid of lesbians, so I'm never surprised when people hold us at a circumspect distance. I don't like it that our sons have to live with that and that they have to work so hard to prove their worth, but they do.

Part of our challenge is to help our sons learn to love themselves so deeply that no one will ever be able to rock their core. They need to know that they are entitled to the best the world has to give and they need to know how to demand it. We want to teach them how to channel anger so it doesn't eat them up. We want to help them learn how to advocate for themselves at school so that they will learn a truer version of history.

There has been debate about whether black children should be nurtured or toughened when they are little, in order to help them with all that lies ahead. We have chosen to love and protect our sons, but we are also arming them with honest information so they won't have unrealistic expectations. We try to be there for our sons and encourage them to keep fighting their fights.

Some people might say that I'm just another white woman who has no business rearing children of color, or that my expectations are unrealistic. People fear that we're raising warriors. Personally I will feel honored if our children have enough spirit and strength and hope to become the freedom fighters or visionaries or leaders of their generation. I will be honored if their presence on earth contributes in any way toward positive social change.

ERIC DEMARCO

I was already fourteen when my mom and I got to know Bonnie. I saw right away how happy Mom was with her, and I hoped she would stay around. Bonnie helped me with homework, listened to my problems, gave me rides, and taught me many things. We all laughed together a lot. I learned to trust her and eventually saw her as my other mom. I always liked the idea of becoming a family, and I always wanted a brother or sister. I only wish I could have had one sooner.

I'm proud of my family. My moms helped me to understand women, and they are good to talk to about girl problems. They taught me that violence begets violence, and that everyone deserves respect. They helped me to learn to respect myself. I know they will always be there for me.

I think it's cool that one of my moms is black and the other is white. There's no room for racism in our family. That's how it should be.

THE BODHI FAMILY

Epi Bodhi · Charlie Bodhi · Gabe (19) · Maya (15)

EPI

When I told my parents that I was going to marry Charlie, my father thought my marriage was my own business, but my mom didn't accept it at first. I never thought it would be a lasting break with her, and I was right. Once my mother accepted my marriage, she was a real champion of it. She would force people she knew to acknowledge us. "This is my son-in-law," she'd announce with pride.

Charlie and I didn't get married to make any kind of political statement, but many years ago our whole family went to a Martin Luther King Jr. Day breakfast. On the way home, Gabe said, "In a way, Mom, we're sort of living Martin Luther King's dream." That was very powerful for me. Charlie and I certainly didn't set out to do it, but I think it's true.

We're just a family, and it makes me feel somewhat exposed to have people look at us as *Other*, as if there's something odd about us. We've been married for twenty years, and I would say that, just as in other marriages, 90 percent of any difficulties we've had, have come from the fact that we're different genders, not races!

> *"I've often thought that looking white is almost a disguise where I can hear what people think about the other side. There shouldn't be another side, but unfortunately, I have to live in a world where there are two sides."*
> *—Gabe Bodhi*

CHARLIE

I grew up in an unusual family. In order to try and shield us kids from the impact of racism, my folks always used to talk about "C" and "W" when they were talking about people. Of course, us kids picked up pretty quickly that they were meaning, "Colored" and "White."

In our society, whenever we look at any other person, the first thing we see is race. And along with that seeing come certain assumptions about that person. We think we know something about the kind of music and food that person likes, the kind of home that person comes from. We need to begin challenging those assumptions.

When white people find out that our children, Gabe and Maya, come from a mixed background, they have to reexamine their assumptions. Because our kids "look white," the white observers have to say, "Wait a second. Gabe looks just like me. What does that say about my background? Or the background of my friends? Or of my spouse?"

I understand why some African American women feel that I've sold out by marrying a white woman. I know where it's coming from because, as African American people, we've had to stay together to move forward, and there's strength and protection in numbers. To have moved away from my race, in a sense, means abandonment. On the other hand, I have to resist any form of police mentality. Who is going to define for me who I am, who I can love, and what I can do?

GABE

From nursery school to about fourth grade, race and appearance wasn't an issue. Kids cared only about who was the most fun to play with. When the other kids started noticing and pointing out that my father was black and that I wasn't just what I appeared to be, it was a hard change for me.

One of the most significant events in my childhood was traveling down South. I had this huge fear that the Ku Klux Klan was going to drag us all off. The Confederate flags all over the place really scared me.

I didn't get any racist comments in junior and senior high. Every once in a while, someone would make a joke about race, without hatred or spite behind it. Like a black kid might say, "Hey, you should be able to dance better because you're black." Or a white kid would joke, "How come you're not better at basketball?"

As a group, multiracial people are very poorly defined. For any minority to be able to move forward, they need to be in the public eye. I now see multiracial women and men in modeling, music, acting, and sports—Hallie Berry, Mariah Carey, Paula Abdul, for example. These people are out there bringing positive attention to multiracial people and to the richness of our dual heritage.

I've often thought that looking white is almost a disguise where I can hear what people think about the other side. There shouldn't be another side, but, unfortunately, I have to live in a world where there are two sides. I do think that I have an obligation to protect who I am and who my family is. When I hear antiblack and antiwhite comments, I try to ease these tensions by telling people about both sides. I confront both the white kids and the black kids.

MAYA

I was seven when our family went down South. It was my first awareness that our family wasn't "normal." We were walking into a store, and my mom said, "Stay close to me because people might look at us weird." I didn't understand why she was saying that. Then she told me it was because they didn't see that many multiracial families in the South. I didn't understand, and it was frightening. I had never had any warning before.

We did a study about South Africa and apartheid in my elementary school—a predominantly white private school where I was the only one in my class with African ancestry. I asked the other kids, "If I went to South Africa, how would they treat me?" Everyone in the class agreed that the white South Africans would treat me fine because I look white, but if they found out that I was half black, they would hate me. That helped me to understand that racism has to do with ideas people have in their head. It didn't matter if my skin was lighter than their skin, I could still be discriminated against. Racism is very confusing!

I was bat mitzvahed. I like the idea of being part of a group of people joined together by a religion. Being biracial and coming from two backgrounds, I don't identify with only one of them. But being Jewish, I enjoy a sense of history and connection.

THE COLER FAMILY

Ming Coler · Andrew Coler · Man-Chin Chung
Wai-Je (10) · Mai Ya (8) · Marga (7) · Hannah (5)

MING

I'm the only one in my family to marry someone of another culture. In my mind, I never have had any racist problems. I grew up in Taiwan, and I came here. If I met a man who was very kind, then that is what I wanted. I never placed race in front of me. I was concerned though about Andrew's age when we first met. I didn't want to marry someone really younger than me. Andrew said he was twenty-two, and I thought, well I'm twenty-four so that's fine. He was really just twenty-one.

I feel that I'm American really. I look in the mirror and say, "Maybe not." But I don't feel different. I just see all people the same way. I don't look at Andrew or the kids as white, or black, or yellow. I look at him as my husband. I see them as my children.

ANDREW

My parents raised me in a nonbiased environment. They didn't teach me stereotypes at an early age. I met Ming at work and fell in love quickly. I said, "Why don't you marry me?" Ming was on a swing. She stopped swinging and said, "Our kids would be so beautiful." We married only six weeks after we had fallen in love.

Some people don't believe in intermarriage, but I strongly disagree. I think the more you break those rules, the more people will have a more open attitude. Why place value or judgment on color? We have to teach people and, in order to teach, we have to set examples.

There are a lot of positive experiences that go with being in a multiracial family. For the children, it's obvious that when you bring two cultures together, you

"Some people don't believe in intermarriage, but I strongly disagree. I think the more you break those rules, the more people will have a more open attitude. Why place value or judgment on color? We have to teach people, and in order to teach, we have to set examples."
—Andrew Coler

21

have more to share and to exchange. They are exposed to the language, the culture, and the society from both ends of the spectrum. It's much easier for them to grow up in a nonbiased way. And, as for me, I've also gotten to know a great deal about the Chinese culture.

The flip side is that there's going to be a culture clash. Ming and I had a period where we fought and fought. I think our conflicts were mainly cultural conflicts—the way a woman who grew up in Taiwan might raise children versus the way a white American early-childhood educator, who's supposed to be an expert, might raise children. But if you pull yourself through it, you'll come out ahead.

THE CROSBY/TILLMAN FAMILY

Janet Crosby · Ivy Tillman · Martin Crosby (3)

JANET

Not long after my mother died, I decided to adopt a baby. When my father heard that I was adopting a black baby, he gave me a few minutes of trouble. I made it clear that I wouldn't listen to that anymore, and that was the end of it. From the moment Martin arrived, my dad has adored him.

There are times when I can't deal with other people's racist behavior. I was in a restaurant with Martin and a little boy came in and hit Martin. His parents said, "Don't do that." And the boy said, "He scares me. Help! Help!" I was too tired that night to spend any time trying to educate the child or the family. I just said, "Martin, come here," and put him on my lap, and we ate our supper.

I wanted a black child. I think there will be times when I will fall short on teaching Martin about black culture, and Ivy will help me in those times.

IVY

I grew up down South, but when I was fifteen I was sponsored by a Northern church, and I moved in with a white family in upstate New York. It was the first time I had ever been around white people at all. I don't think I'd ever seen a white person before. Well, maybe passing on the street. I wasn't expecting them to be any different from me. What was shocking was that they *were* different from me, and that they looked at me as different from them.

Janet and I live together, and we parent together. We're an extended family of friends. I'm planning on adopting a child too, and we will co-parent that child too as a sibling for Martin.

> "If people see us all together, they think Martin is just my child until he calls Janet, 'Momma.' A little girl at the beach asked Janet how she could be his mom because their skin colors were different."
>
> —Ivy Tillman

If people see us all together, they think Martin is just my child until he calls Janet, "Momma." Some little girl at the beach asked Janet how she could be his mom because their skin colors were different.

I will be able to take Martin into the black community in a way that Janet will not be able to because she is different. Because I'm the same, I can take him where she can't.

THE DENIG FAMILY

Bob Denig · Nancy Denig · Julia (12) · Nick (11)

NANCY

Bob and I were living in Germany when we decided to adopt. The social worker asked us if we would be open to adopting nonwhite children. In the best sense, we didn't care one way or the other. We just wanted kids.

While living in Europe, our young children were world citizens and people responded to them that way—most people were not able to figure out what their particular nationality was. On numerous occasions, Nick was surrounded by children wanting to admire and kiss him. In Germany, they were often admired as well, especially for their *schwartze augen*, or beautiful dark eyes.

Being in this family has given me a uniquely personal opening into the diversity of American culture. For example, when I'm out with the kids and we see African Americans, I often see an openness to me as a person, rather than an attitude of, "Who is this white woman?"

Once when Julia was seven, she blurted out, "I wish I weren't brown," and then she spilled out a story about a little girl calling her names at school. I said, "Julia, there's no problem with you. The problem is with this girl, and I feel sorry for a girl who talks to people this way. It's *her* problem." After talking about this, Julia really changed. She realized that it was fine to be just the way she was. But it will not always be so easy to comfort her and Nick in the midst of our society's racial sickness. By helping them find their own inner strength, we hope it will help.

The best part for Bob and for me of being in a multiracial family is that we have our children, and we adore them. We didn't adopt our children because of a mission, but now—given who we are as a family—we have a mission to be part of some healing in our culture.

"I'm not being colorblind—we are who we are—but the best thing about our family is that we are together."
—Bob Denig

BOB

Part of our family history is that we went through seven years of wanting kids very much and not having them. It was really painful for us, and our families shared the pain. They were delighted and excited when we adopted Julia and Nick.

Our parents did wonder whether people would accept our kids. Nancy and I kind of blew it off. We told our parents, "C'mon, get with it!" We had left America in 1979 when it seemed like racial issues were moving in a positive direction. But the America we came back to with the kids in 1984 was a really different place than we thought it would be. It was clear that racism had become much more socially acceptable once again.

When we were about to adopt our kids, the idea that they were biracial seemed important to me. At least, I thought, Nancy and I shared half of their heritage. Now, it doesn't seem all that important. In the last couple of years, I mostly refer to our kids as African American or black because as far as the world is concerned, they are black. Also, the fact that they have white parents and live in a predominantly white culture, inevitably they are going to tap into plenty of white stuff. It's the African American stuff that needs to be nurtured.

26

Last summer, I visited an Episcopal Church summer camp every week because I'm the bishop in this area. A group of teen-aged African American girls were talking about this really cool kid at camp named Nick. I said, "I know Nick." They were surprised. "You know Nick?" I said, "Not only do I know him, I live with him. . . . *Nick's my son*." They said, "What? No!!" When they finally believed me, they said, "Oh, that's why he does the prayers so well at the service!"

Nick's standard compliment for a long time whenever I did something good was, "Not too bad for a white guy!"

We set out to have children, and I really love the children we have. The fact that they are African American is an important part of who they are and an important part of who we are as a family. But what really stands out is that we are these four individuals who by God's grace, or by serendipity, or by dumb luck are thrown together and are spending our lives together. Somehow that seems more important than the racial issues. I'm not being colorblind—we are who we are—but the best thing about our family is that *we* are together.

JULIA

I was reading *Gone with the Wind* and lots of long books by C.S. Lewis and E.B. White in third grade. These books were way over my age level, and yet I was getting "C's" in reading. The teacher's excuse to my parents was, "Julia reads so fast, I don't know if she knows what she's reading," even though I could answer all her questions about the books.

This white girl was in line with me at school and she was taunting me by saying, "Blackie. Brownie. Blackie. Brownie." I told the teacher, and she called the girl's mom and the mom got mad at the girl. The girl apologized to me and gave me some Hershey kisses and cookies. We became friends.

I don't really see us as a multiracial family. I just see us as a family. Families like ours aren't really that uncommon. There were two other black kids with white parents at my school last year.

NICK

An African American woman who is married to a white man told me that you get more knowledge out of being in a multiracial family, and that you will do well in life knowing different things about African American people and white people. I agree with her.

THE ELSASSER/ROBINSON FAMILY

Michael Elsasser · Doug Robinson · Justin Robinson (9)
Zachary Robinson (7)

MICHAEL

Doug and I met about fourteen years ago on a stalled subway train underneath the East River in Manhattan. We became good friends and then partners. I moved in with Doug about seven years ago. Doug had already adopted Justin, and I was his godfather. There was a transition time when I had to become "Poppy" to Justin. He was two then, and I think it took about a year.

We got a phone call two years later from a child welfare agency. They said they thought they had the perfect child for us, and they did. Soon after, Zach joined our family. Doug, Justin and I brought him in to make the four of us a family.

When people see us, some of them say, "Oh look, there's a gay couple, and I have problems with gay couples." Or, "Oh, there's an interracial couple, and I have problems with interracial relationships." We strike up a lot of interest as a family because we touch other people's fears and prejudices just by our existence. In terms of who we are and how we see ourselves, this is just our family.

DOUG

Family is very important to me. It wasn't important for me to have biological kids, just to have kids. I also had grown up in a family where giving back to the community was very important, so I decided to adopt children from the foster care system. In New York City where we live, and throughout the country, the majority of children in the foster care system are African American or Hispanic. I guess the rest is history. We have two beautiful boys. In our home, they flourish and bloom.

Mike and I could not see living without children. It's a wonderful experience to see new life and to watch the boys develop and mature. Watching Justin walk

> *"When people see us, some of them say, 'Oh look, there's a gay couple, and I have problems with gay couples.' Or, 'Oh, there's an interracial couple, and I have problems with interracial relationships.' We strike up a lot of interest as a family because we touch other people's fears and prejudices just by our existence. In terms of who we are and how we see ourselves, this is just our family."*
> *—Michael Elsasser*

was amazing because he walked at such an early age. He was only ten months old and an incredible walker! And Zachary at two years old was standing on his head! We loved being there on the day each of them learned to ride their bicycles.

Our family life is a very traditional American family life—early morning getting up, eating breakfast, getting dressed, making sure everyone has matching socks, getting the boys off to school, and then going to work. At night, it's homework and getting ready for bed. Weekends, I coach Justin's soccer team. We've been class parents in Zach's and Justin's classes every single year. We feel we want to be there for our children all the time.

I always draw parallels between my experience growing up in the fifties and sixties as an African American, and being gay in America in the nineties. Our family was the first one to integrate the town I grew up in. My brothers were the first black kids to join the YMCA. People thought that everything was going to go haywire—that all the work the white community had done to make our town a community would all go downhill when the blacks integrated it. But after meeting us and figuring out who we were, it wasn't the big deal that some people made it to be. I think it's the same thing with us gay people—it's not a big deal. We're just like everybody else.

JUSTIN

My name is Justin Tyler Robinson, and I'm in the fifth grade. We go to our grandparents' house to visit. Our cousins live down the road. We play baseball and soccer, and our dads coach our teams.

A family is people who love each other.

ZACHARY

My name is Zachary Maurice Robinson, and I'm going into second grade. I want to go to the Bronx Zoo. We went to see the Mets play baseball. I always make the beds. I clean up our bedroom; Justin cleans up the playroom.

A family is . . . well, I live with my dads and the big guy—my brother—and our puppy, Yondo.

THE FORD FAMILY

Janet Obermann Ford · Richard Ford · Kristen (6) · Aaron (10)

JANET

Growing up in an all white, Protestant, middle-class suburb left me numb to cultural differences. I was raised not to be bigoted in any way, but I was totally ignorant of people who were unlike me. That left me unaware, and at times afraid or suspicious of anyone different than myself.

I had no friends of color until I was in graduate school. Then I fell in love with Richard, a black-skinned, blue-eyed, multiracial African American. I married him because I loved him, but I had no idea how the differences in our racial and cultural backgrounds would impact on our lives. We felt we had enough similarities at the "core" of ourselves to bind us together. We've weathered many storms and done an incredible amount of growing over the past twelve years.

This summer our family visited Ellis Island. I was moved by the realization that my own great-grandfather, at the age of ten, was among the masses of European immigrants who waited in the great reception hall at Ellis Island. I tried to visualize the very different circumstances in which some of Richard's relatives came to this country. I was forced to contemplate the fact that some of my childrens' distant relatives came to this country aboard ships carrying a "cargo" of slaves.

It's more painful being in a multiracial marriage because I'm often forced to look at issues that I'd really rather not think about. It's probably easier to be married to someone of the same race, culture, or creed because you're not constantly reminded of your own culture's one-mindedness.

I believe that children raised in multicultural and multiracial families are blessed with a cultural intelligence and sensitivity that children of single-race families can rarely achieve.

Multiracial families develop a sense of "being in the middle." When we lived in the South, our family went to the annual Fourth of July celebration. Reflecting

"Our children consider themselves mixed, and they have a pride in their multiracial heritage. In the end, however, racial identity becomes an unnecessary construct. We are all part of the human race."

—Richard Ford

31

the legacy of slavery, the blacks were all on one side of the square while the whites were gathered on the other side. There was a clear division of race and culture, even in the types of music being played on each "side" and the types of food being served! Aaron, who was six years old then, asked me, "Where do we belong Mommy?" We spent our day meandering between both crowds of people, never feeling comfortable or welcomed in either setting. That day I realized that we would not raise our children in the South, and that we would have to be selective in where we chose to live.

It's not easy to be a multiracial family, but I am proud of who the Fords are.

RICHARD

We've been married for twelve years, and every week there has been some reaction to us being together. These range from curious stares to the more rare hostile expressions of anger at our relationship.

Since there has always been racial diversity in my family, Janet was welcomed warmly and quickly. She has become a sister to my sisters and is closer to them now than I am.

The political implications of our marriage are real. The racism in this country has always put white womanhood on a higher level than other women. Janet and I represent a marriage that can be condemned as just another highly educated black man united with a white woman. People often wonder whether I married Janet because I am more attracted to white women or because, regardless of her race, I found her to be loveable.

If my children look white can they really be black? I feel good about using the word "biracial" too. Our children consider themselves mixed, and they have pride in their multiracial heritage. In the end, however, racial identity becomes an unnecessary construct. We are all part of the human race.

THE FRIEDLANDER/GOLDSCHEIDER FAMILY

Debbi Friedlander · Eric Goldscheider · Joshua (3)

DEBBI

Joshua was two when we adopted him in Jamaica, and we're still in contact with his birthmother. She was worried about whether Joshua would be around any black people where we live. I told her that there were many other families like ours who belonged to a multiracial family group, and that we planned to join when we got home.

As soon as we decided to adopt a child of another race, we realized how much the media is racially slanted. Being of the dominant race, you don't really notice it so much. When your family is multiracial, you notice it all the time.

Joshua looked at my hands and then at his, and he said, "Our skins are different." And I said, "Yup, that's right. What's different about our skins?" He said "Mine is brown." And then I said, "Yes, and mine is pink, but we both have hands, and we both have skin." This started a whole thing of talking about all kinds of things that are different and the same. "My bicycle is different from yours, and my bicycle is the same as yours."

ERIC

I lived in Africa for a year, and when we started to think about adopting—I don't know why—I wanted to adopt a black child and be a multiracial family.

When we first decided to adopt a black child, I told my father. He said, "Wouldn't you want to consider adopting an Asian child because their I.Q. is higher?" Of course, I argued with him about his racist stereotypes. When Joshua was two and a half, I took him to visit my dad for the first time. Joshua picked up the spoons on the dining table, and my father's wife said, "Oh look, he's already trying to steal the silverware."

A five-year-old girl told Joshua that she was going to a county fair and that

> "When I took Joshua for a medical exam, there was a registration card which asked about the race of the child. The nurse filled in, 'white.' When I saw it, I said to her, 'Josh isn't white. He's black.' Because he was with me, I guess she didn't even think about it."
>
> —Eric Goldscheider

35

black people couldn't go to that fair. Only white people could go. Of course, her parents corrected her. Later on in the day, Joshua was playing a game. He said to the little girl, "This is something only black people can do. White people can't do it."

It crosses my mind that someday Joshua might say to me, "I don't like you because you're white." I don't know how to prepare for it. I just will have to go with it if it happens. I have a feeling that it's something he will try out at some time, to see what the effect is.

When I took Josh for a medical exam, there was a registration card which asked about the race of the child. The nurse filled in "white." When I saw it, I said, "Josh isn't white. He's black." Because he was with me, I guess she didn't even think about it.

THE GERSHUNY/WEISS FAMILY

Diane Gershuny · Richard Weiss · Zoë (4)

DIANE

I knew I wanted to adopt a baby girl from China the moment I found out that I could. It felt right for me from the very beginning.

My family didn't seem to have any problem with the adoption, maybe because some of my relatives have Asian features. However, I never felt that how she looked would matter. In fact, it bothers me a bit when people tell me how much Zoë looks like me as if that makes our relationship "better," or "more natural."

I want very much for Zoë to be proud of her rich ethnic heritage, but I also want her to someday understand the social, economic and political conditions existing in China at the time of her birth.

If her birth parents knew that Zoë was deaf, they surely knew that being adopted would probably be her only chance to be educated. Only a very small percentage of deaf children in China receive an education. Zoë's birth parents obviously made a very painful, but wise, choice.

When people find out that Zoë is hearing-impaired, they focus more on that than on the fact that we're of different races. I guess it's more common where we live to be adopted and Asian than it is to be deaf and have a cochlear implant.

Zoë and our family are unique in many ways and I know that there will be many times when she wishes she were "like everyone else." Yet, I think that with all the love and support she's receiving now, she'll grow up feeling comfortable and secure no matter where she is in the world.

RICHARD

I never give it much thought that Zoë is a different race from mine. Perhaps it's because I live in New York City where there are many Asian people and people of all ethnicities and races rather than a majority of one ethnic group.

"It bothers me a bit when people tell me how much Zoë looks like me, as if that makes our relationship 'better' or 'more natural.'"

—Diane Gershuny

When I take Zoë out of the apartment, people sometimes give us a "double take." I assume they are thinking that we don't look anything alike.

I enjoy taking Zoë to Chinatown so that she can experience more people of her own culture and race. The people seem to be more open to me and show particular interest in Zoë.

THE HARPER/JOHNSON FAMILY

Marilyn Harper · David Johnson
Diana (15) · Sam (10) · Elizabeth (4) · Emily (4)

MARILYN

I had applied as a single parent to adopt a baby before I married David. So, David knew before we got married that adoption was going to be part of our family plan.

Once we were married, we began trying to adopt a child who was biracial. Not long after that, Sam's birth family chose David and me to adopt Sam. Because we were an interracial couple, Sam's birth father thought that our family was the ideal place for a Korean child to be raised. Sam came to us when he was two years old. When we decided to adopt a second time, another birth family chose us to parent their child for the same reason. So, we adopted Elizabeth when she was an infant. She's Guatemalan.

When we made the decision to adopt a third time, we wanted to adopt an older child in the toddler stage. We had gone through the baby stages, and we didn't want to do that again! We contacted an agency, and they said that they had a child who was perfect for our family. This child was Hispanic. However, when they found out I was African American, they said they would never place a child who was not black or part black with a black or interracial family because it wasn't fair to the child. This same agency places black children with white families.

I decided our third child was going to be Caucasian. I called it an "in-your-face adoption." I wanted to show that it was doable, that an African American person can parent a white child and can do a good job of it. So we ended up flying to Russia to adopt Emily. She was two when she came home. Just recently, our teen-age daughter, Diana, joined our family.

When we adopted Sam and Elizabeth, it was an easy decision to make. They were kids of color. The decision to adopt Emily was a harder decision to make

"It's not possible to be colorblind. If you don't see the color of your kids that means that you're not really seeing them or accepting them for who they are."
—Marilyn Harper

because she was a white child, and not only white, but blonde and blue-eyed. I wondered if I was prepared for the negative feedback I would get. I wondered if there would be backlash from the African American community. I imagined them saying, "Why did Marilyn do this when there are so many African American kids waiting?"

I haven't heard anything negative yet. All of my thirteen siblings have been very supportive. My father happens to be biracial—his mother was white—and there are a number of interracial marriages in my family. So my family was very accepting of the adoptions. It was a non-issue. I think that ideally the best place for children is in same-race placements, but if a same-race placement cannot be found quickly, then I think a transracial placement is a good choice.

I kept hearing African American social workers with their slogan that "Love is not enough." And I agree that love is not enough, but I think it's a big part of the equation. If kids do have love, all the other things they need can be met. The black social workers felt that whites couldn't teach black kids about racism and, in a way, they can't. But I think these parents can be taught and can learn, and I don't think kids should stay in foster homes or group homes because a same-race placement isn't there. Kids shouldn't wait.

The bill that President Clinton just signed says the very same thing, that same-race placements have preference, but kids shouldn't languish in foster care for months or years waiting for that to happen. If you can't find a same-race placement for a child in three months, then you can look for transracial placement. I support that.

I'm from a rural Louisiana small town with less than one thousand people where things are very separate. Blacks live on one side of town, whites on the other. Churches are totally segregated. I went to a 100 percent African American university, so up until I began teaching, there was no integration in my life. I would never have dreamed that this family would have happened to me.

Once you are parenting children of different races, then you can see much more clearly that the race issue has so little to do with everyday life. It is not the biggie you once thought it would be. We do things to help the kids learn about their culture, but it's not the end-all of everything.

Still, it's not possible to be colorblind. If you say you don't see the color of your kids, then you're not really seeing them or accepting them for who they are.

When we go places, I always feel like I'm on stage because we're always conspicuous. When I'm out with the kids, people are always looking, wondering, or saying something like, "Oh I see you have a big group today." They assume I'm baby-sitting, and people have asked if I'm the nanny. I've had instances at the mall when Emily was crying and a security guard approached me and thought I was kidnapping her. Those kinds of things happen, but that just goes with the territory.

The negatives of my family structure are so small. They are just the little things like people staring at us, and I try not to let this bother me. Even when people ask me if I'm the nanny, I just kind of laugh it off because how often do you see an African American person with a kid like Emily? I can understand people making this mistake, so unless they are rude after I tell them, it's fine. If you see a white man with a full-black child, you might automatically assume that the child is adopted because it's so much more common. But with my situation—with Asian and white and Hispanic children—people just don't assume it's possible.

The best thing for me has been meeting people, like people in the Russian and

Korean communities—meeting people I would never have had contact with. And the kids are also learning about their cultures in different adoption support groups.

In the African American community, my children are embraced. Yet, I think about the tensions blacks and Koreans have had. We were recently at a wedding, and Sam was the only Asian kid among hundreds of African American kids, and he was having a grand time with all of them. I thought that this was great for him to have a family which is African American and to be able to socialize and get along. I think, in the long run, to be able to interact with all these people is going to be to their betterment.

DAVID

It opens your eyes to see all these racial issues. I grew up in a rural area, where there were supposedly no racial issues. There weren't any major racial issues because there was no diversity. Everybody was basically from the same ethnic group—Germans and Norwegians. If they weren't actually related, they were from the same culture. If African Americans passed by, the repercussions were felt for fifteen miles around. Everyone knew about it.

When we adopted our children, my parents were very accepting, just like Marilyn's family. We spend a lot of time at their home most holidays, and they visit us often. Other extended family members have been accepting, too.

News articles were never written about our family when we just had Sam and Elizabeth, but when Emily came, reporters were very interested in us. It was more exotic to have a black mother and a white daughter, so we became famous for adopting kids from all over the world.

When I'm out with the children by myself, I get virtually no comments. People are so accustomed to seeing European Americans with transracially adopted children. It's considered "old hat." When Marilyn tells me about her experiences, mine are so vastly different. I blend in instead of standing out.

SAM

I don't see any differences. We're just a family like everybody else. I like to go fishing with Dad, go on picnics, go to movies, swim. And I like going to Grandma's house.

When I was in elementary school, kids would tease me and make slanted eyes and call me "Chinese."

I take pride in being Korean because I'm different from other people. If we were all the same, it would be so boring. I like being Korean because Asians seem well respected and other people have high expectations of us.

ELIZABETH

I like to go on picnics, go to the zoo, go to the park, and go to Grandma's house.

THE HIAM FAMILY

Heather Hiam · Alex Hiam · Eliot (8) · Paul (6) · Noelle (1)

HEATHER

My father was black and my mother was white. When I was a kid, we knew four or five other interracial families, and we used to get together with them often. When I was in fifth grade we moved to a white suburb where I was the only black child at school. Sometimes I was the target of name-calling. The name-calling was always about being black.

My parents told me and my siblings that people who used insulting names to describe other people were not the kind of folks we would ever want to be friends with. We were told to completely ignore people who said things that hurt our feelings. My parents tried to create a world within our family that was distinctly apart from many mainstream social attitudes and values.

My parents made a strong effort to make my brother, my sister, and me identify ourselves as black rather than biracial because in a racist society we would always be considered black.

When my brother was twenty, he ended up having his nose broken while defending an acquaintance who had been called a racial epithet. Despite the trauma, we were proud of him.

Generally, black people know that I'm black, but white people often don't know for sure. Those who try to figure out my background guess everything from Polynesian to Greek. When I'm working in China, people often ask whether I'm from Xinjiang, where the people have green eyes like mine. And when Alex, Noelle, and I went to our first multiracial family group dinner party, a white man asked me in a friendly way why our family was there. He thought our entire family was white.

A close friend of mine who is black and was married to a white man during the 1970s got a divorce largely because she felt a desire to be part of the black community. She has since regretted it, saying, " We loved each other, and that is

> *"I think that people have great difficulty getting along with each other, so any little pockets of harmony—amid all the discord—are foundations on which the future can be built."*
> —Alex Hiam

45

all that really matters. I've never found anyone else who values me as much as he did." I've taken her experience to heart, and try to keep in mind that the chance to be with someone who really cares about you doesn't happen all that often. We need to cherish those opportunities.

It's interesting to see how people can have different skin colors in the same family. Our son Eliot has identified himself as black since he was three. Paul's skin is much lighter, and he recently said that he wanted to have darker skin to look more like Eliot. He said he felt left out because Eliot's skin color is nearer to mine. I don't think it would make much sense for Paul to identify himself as black. It's great that there are more biracial people around, and that the word "biracial" is becoming an option. I hope Paul uses it.

ALEX

I came from conservative white families on both sides, and my marriage to Heather is very much of an anomaly. It occurred to me that marrying a black woman might cause a lot of friction, but it never really did. That's to their credit, I suppose.

I do remember when Eliot was born my parents' first two questions were, "Is it a boy or a girl?" and, "What does he *look* like?" They knew that their grandchildren could be any color. And, in fact, Eliot is dark-skinned, and Paul and Noelle are light-skinned. It forces you to abandon the myth of race.

Not everybody approves of multiracial families, so I've been very pleased that our children haven't experienced anything serious yet in the way of problems. Honestly, it's probably because we have avoided the parts of the country where that might be the case. There are very few communities that I'd be willing to bring my children up in.

When we were about to become parents, we talked about all the possible issues associated with being multiracial. Will our kids have problems identifying themselves? Will they experience some prejudice or confusion about friends, groups, cliques? To me, those problems are less important than the benefits. In a way, it's a gift to be able to tell the kids that they not only have white and black blood, but they have Irish, Scottish, English, African, and even Native American blood from Heather's great-grandmother. The kids really represent a lot of traditions and backgrounds. They can carry on the best of all of them.

I saw a century-old census form, and the instructions for the person administering it had the most elaborate, detailed section on how to determine what per-

46

centage black each person was. In one hundred years, I think that a lot of those attitudes have changed, but not completely. It's still a racist society, so I think it's important to raise a multiracial kid to know that there is part of society that says, "If you have any black blood in you, you're black." So a biracial kid shouldn't say, "Well, since I'm only half black, maybe I should just call myself white." That exercise is unproductive.

You can't solve race problems through having multiracial children. In fact, you might view being multiracial as a burden for children who have to bear their parents' ideals. You end up passing your ideals on without having cleared it with your children in advance. But I don't think that it's a problem. I think it's a strength.

I think that people have great difficulty getting along with each other, so any little pockets of harmony—amid all the discord—are foundations on which the future can be built.

PAUL

I don't think our family is different from other families. It just seems the same. We do the same things everybody else does. But to other people it's not very usual. No one I know at school is multiracial.

If people think I look white, then that's what I am to them. I don't think about other people's race. People might look different facially, but their race doesn't really matter to me.

THE HILYARD FAMILY

Gail Young Hilyard · Stephen Hilyard · Jeremy (8)

GAIL

I was raised in the South by my grandmother. She talked very little about the oppression of racism, but our roles were well defined. We blacks knew our place, and I knew it wasn't right. As a child, I wanted to know about *all* people. At thirteen, I really hungered for this coming together of all people because I couldn't believe that God would leave us like this. Then I was introduced to the Bahai faith. Bahais believe that there is only one race—the human race. They encourage interracial marriages to improve race relations.

If only people could realize that we are all created equally, that every person has the same desires and wants, and that all people come from the same stock, we would be witnessing heaven on earth. When you marry someone of another race, you really understand all that.

One of the blessings of being in an interracial marriage is that you find out that it isn't about race—rather, it's about how you treat and respect one another. For me, it gets down to who's going to do those dishes, who's going to pick up Jeremy at school. It's the day-to-day routine which we deal with in our marriage. It's funny, but most people haven't made that connection.

If you get into an interracial relationship, you should study the history and culture of your partner's race. It was extremely important to me for Stephen to know about the continuous struggles of African Americans in this country.

The most difficult thing for us as an interracial couple has been the parenting of our child. There are values that I was brought up with which are very different from Stephen's. Stephen was raised with a sense of freedom and exploration, whereas I was not. Certain things Jeremy would say or do would be considered disrespectful by me—whereas to Stephen, the same things would be considered "expressing one's opinion."

I think all children should live in a diverse setting, especially those from mul-

"If only people could realize that we are all created equally, that every person has the same desires and wants, and that all people come from the same stock, we would be witnessing heaven on earth."
—Gail Hilyard

49

tiracial families. It probably doesn't matter so much when they are little, but then the child grows up and looks around and says, "No one looks like me or my family." A child needs more than love. Along with love, you want the child to be proud of all parts of their racial heritage. And where you live should reflect it.

We don't just talk about the oneness of mankind in our family, we live it. This weekend we're having "Puerto Rican Night." Last month we had "Russian Night." We ask people of different backgrounds to cook at our house. We talk together about their culture, we eat their food, look at pictures of their country, and play their music. Jeremy sees this, and it anchors him.

Jeremy is able to move between all races of people; he just slides in and out. As a young child, Jeremy has already realized that there's really only one race—the human race. For me, it took to my late teens to understand that concept. Jeremy is way ahead.

STEVE

My background is very different from Gail's. I grew up in a town where there were only three black families. I saw some diversity in the colleges nearby, and when I was thirteen I began going to different cultural festivals. From these events, I got to know people from all over the world. When you come from a very homogeneous place, anything different is exciting.

I was in the Peace Corps in the West Indies where I experienced being in the minority for the first time. There were people who liked me because I was American, and people who disliked me because I was American. Both attitudes made me uncomfortable because I felt that I wasn't being treated as an individual.

Maybe if Jeremy grows up seeing his dad making human mistakes, he won't ever feel intimidated by white people.

THE HUBBARD FAMILY

Maki Hubbard · Jamie Hubbard · Christopher (11) · Alicia (6)

MAKI

When I first met Jamie in Japan, my mother said, "Don't bring a foreigner over to our house." But when she met Jamie formally, and he was speaking Japanese, and he knew more about Buddhism than she did, she was overwhelmed and impressed. Now she listens to him more than to me!

Some people ask how it is to be married to an American, and I really have to think about it because, in a way, I've never thought of Jamie as being American. It wasn't a negative or positive factor in my decision to marry him. Every time a person says, "Oh, wow, you are a multiracial family," we look at each other and say, *"We are?"*

Of course, Jamie and I are different. With certain things I just can't compromise—like putting soy sauce or butter on the rice, or muddy shoes in the bedroom. But Jamie doesn't do those things—well, sometimes he puts soy sauce on his rice if he cooks and it isn't a Japanese dinner.

I wouldn't have married somebody who said, "Oh, you are Japanese. Would you make me some chow mein?" But Jamie knows the language and understands Japanese people. I think that helps.

It would be nice in the future if this world becomes a place where our children don't have to worry whether they are Japanese or American. I don't want to impose my identity on my children. I know this goes against the trendy thing, but I don't really care about "roots" consciousness. To cling to a cultural or racial identity is to miss all of the other possibilities of the whole world, and is the obvious cause of a lot of hatred in the world as well. Besides, my own experience tells me that a single, unchanging identity is a false construct anyway.

Because of Alicia's curls and light skin, people often ask if I'm her baby-sitter.

Before I had children, I told Jamie that I wanted to be buried in Japan—that my soul and heart belong to Japan. Looking at my children, I don't feel that way now.

"In Japan, the word for biracial is 'haafu' or 'half.' We stress to Alicia and Christopher that they're not half anything. They've got twice as much as most everyone else—two countries, two cultures, two languages."
—Jamie Hubbard

JAMIE

I grew up in Milwaukee, and I didn't know anyone other than white middle-class Catholics. When I went to study in Japan, my grandmother told me, "You better not bring a Jap home—they're sneaky, you know." I had to show her the dictionary to prove that "Jap" was a derogatory term. But it isn't much different in Japan. When I was dating Maki, her mother thought all foreigners were barbarians, which is not entirely unreasonable, I guess.

A friend said to me, "You and Maki are changing the world. You're breaking down national boundaries, racial boundaries, and cultural boundaries. With your children, you are making citizens of the world." But to tell the truth, Maki and I never had any conscious intention of changing the world or standing up for our ideals.

When we visit Japan, we speak Japanese and it's comfortable for Alicia and Christopher. On the other hand, when we're here, it seems like cruel and unusual punishment to force our children to speak Japanese. My brothers married women who speak other languages, and they tried to raise their children bilingually. But anything that's different, children will get nailed for at school.

My mother doesn't think I'm very American anymore and Maki's not purely Japanese—we're kind of betwixt and between—neither this nor that. So we get to indulge in a fantasy of being global citizens. The feelings toward African Americans in this culture are not the same as they are toward Japanese. We are very lucky.

I don't think there could be any comparison between an interracial black-white relationship and my marriage to Maki. A white male and a Japanese woman are both part of the cultures of power.

It was different when we were kids, but now, to be an eleven-year-old Japanese American kid is power. All the best cars, stereos, and televisions come from Japan. So, our kids have never experienced the kind of difficulty you might expect in multiracial families. In fact, the kids are not put down because of their Japanese American heritage; rather, their friends think it's cool. On top of that is their privileged class background. To our children's friends, "multicultural" means that our kids are jet-setters, going back and forth to Japan so often that they've become blasé about the experience.

I don't know where Alicia got the habit of putting things on rice like salad dressing and soy sauce. Christopher is grossed out by it. He spent his first two years in Japan, and he knows that no Japanese person would ever do that. He thinks brown rice is the pits.

When I asked Alicia if she was Japanese, she said, "No." Then I asked her if she was American and she said, "Not really." Next I said, "Well, what are you?" She answered, "English." Then I asked her if she was a *gaijin,* which means foreigner or white. She said, "No way." Then I asked again if she is Japanese. She said, "No, but I will be when I go back to Japan."

In Japan, the word for biracial is "*haafu*" or "half." We stress to Alicia and Christopher that they're not half anything. They've got twice as much as most everybody else—two countries, two cultures, two languages.

THE KHANNA FAMILY

Lisa Khanna · Ravi Khanna · Anjali (7) · Shyam (5)
Asha Devi (2 months)

LISA

I grew up in a predominantly black neighborhood. My mother worked in the Civil Rights movement, and she started something called the Fair Housing Council.

I met Ravi in India. The thought that the color of our skin or the difference in our cultures would affect our relationship never occurred to me. The whole thing about interracial marriages is that you don't set out to marry someone of a certain color or race, but you marry the person you love.

Ravi and I put off having kids for years because we lived in places where it seemed impossible to raise a child of mixed race. We felt it would be too cruel. We were married ten years before we moved to our present hometown and adopted Anjali from India. Then I gave birth to Shyam and Asha. People from all over the world live in our area. Here, it's very accepted to be in an interracial relationship. It's a complete turnaround for us.

Anjali would like to look like me, but she thinks I should become more brown. She'd like me to wear black eye make-up so my eyes would look more like hers. She always says, "Oh, I wish you were Indian." And Shyam is now completely in love with India and Indian mythology. He asks me, "Don't I look like Daddy?"

Saying that our kids are tolerant is too mild. They truly accept people for who they are. They'll be able to marry whomever they want because they've grown up with family members who aren't the same color as they are. I think they'll feel completely comfortable to follow their hearts.

If you grow up with kids from different countries and races, it's hard to think about having wars with them. If you've known an Iraqi student in your class at school, it's much harder to think of bombing them.

"If you grow up with kids from different countries and races, it's hard to think about having wars with them."
—Lisa Khanna

RAVI

I went to a boarding school with lots of Westerners where I was exposed to many languages and cultures. Then I became an English translator for a spiritual teacher, so I came into contact with many Westerners. I think I would have had difficulty marrying an Indian woman because it would have been very hard to adjust to a traditional Indian family life with arranged marriages and all that.

I see a lot of advantages to being in a multiracial family. It's the way the world is going. Well, actually the world isn't doing very well with everyone killing each other. It's tricky because some people are into having their culture and purity and there's something nice about that in a way, but it can pretty quickly become terrible like so-called ethnic cleansing. My hope is that the world will move toward more blending of cultures and races.

THE KILEY FAMILY

Kathy Kiley · Dan Kiley · Christian (12) · Meg (8)
Olivia (4) · Ben (3) · Sam (3)

KATHY

The political implications of being in a multiracial family are impossible to escape, though in no way did such implications motivate us to adopt our children. In particular, the small vocal group of opponents of the adoptions of black children by white parents has planted a good deal of misinformation into the public consciousness, leading us to defend our family's very existence.

Because multiracial families are a nearly invisible part of the fabric of our society, we helped found a multiracial family group in our area. The group offers a way for our families to support one another and to have a voice.

We are lucky to be enriched by each other, bridging the racial chasm that is so often difficult to cross. For our family, race doesn't take on so much importance that it overshadows the truly important aspects of life—kindness, humanity, respect, and love. We are given, on a daily basis, the opportunity to celebrate race while transcending racial strife. Success in doing so teaches all our children invaluable lessons.

"It's the same being in our multiracial family as being in a family with all the same races except for having different skin color than your brothers and sisters."
—Christian Kiley

DAN

When we adopted Olivia and then the twins, some of our extended family members asked us, "Won't this be too difficult on you? Won't it be too hard on your biological kids?" These reactions were born of fear and the need to protect us. Some of that fear is gone now because our families love our children. They've been able to see the kids not only as children of color but as individuals.

We've faced no earth-shattering racism or discrimination; rather we encounter the almost daily bombardment of little things: rude stares or ignorant questions and comments.

Strangers often question us about our family—at the mall, grocery store, and other public places. We try to react politely with a sense of humor, as Kathy and I stay healthier that way, and we think that attitude will best serve our children. Racism runs rampant, to be sure, and it's often subtle, but many people are genuinely kind, just ill-informed. We've discovered that people in our society don't think all that much about racial issues, and when they do, they seem very confused.

We tend to encounter rude as opposed to mean-spirited people. We would defend our family with stronger verbal reactions if necessary, though.

Our older children don't consider their family particularly unusual, and when outsiders ask them questions or talk about "real" brothers and sisters, it bothers them enough that they set the record straight.

A black man married to a white woman told me that white people who love someone who is black—a spouse or a child—"become black." He feels that his wife has experienced this, and Kathy and I have too. White racism becomes an even more painful, personal affront when its target is someone you love. White people who are intimately involved with black people do indeed begin to understand what it is like to be black.

CHRISTIAN

It's not very different being in a multiracial family until you think of it in the long-term. It will give us experiences we wouldn't have in another family. We will realize what it's like for people of color—it's harder for them. And it's good to realize that.

It's the same being in our multiracial family as a family with all the same races except for having different skin color than your brothers and sisters.

THE LAUFER/WRIGHT FAMILY

Jody Wright · Prakash Laufer · Olisa (13) · Mahajoy (10)
Liina (8) · Emily (2)

JODY

As soon as I had difficulty getting pregnant, I considered adopting a child of a different race. We told everybody we knew that we wanted to adopt because we felt we would be guided to our child in that way. The whole process of adopting our first daughter, Olisa, only took a few months. Her birth mom is Filipino and her birth father is from Zimbabwe. Next we adopted Mahajoy, and her birth mom is also Filipino and her birth father is from Liberia. Then we gave birth to Liina. Our baby Emily is biracial too, and both her birth parents are American.

The grandparents aren't closer to our biological daughter Liina than they are to our adopted daughters. Except once, many years ago, Prakash's mom was talking about her family tree, and she questioned whether our adopted kids were on the family tree or not. I said, "Well, it depends on if your family tree is based on blood or love," and I left the room. When I came back in, his mom said, "You're right," and it hasn't come up again.

We worked really hard at exposing the kids to all their cultures. They came to a point where they said they felt pushed all of the time, so we slowed down for a while. Then Mahajoy started reading about Harriet Tubman at a friend's house. She came home and said, "We should have books like this." I took her into our home library, and showed her a stack of books we already had collected. Now, Mahajoy sings with "Harmony," a multiracial choir group, so she learns a lot about black history in that way too.

Mahajoy got called the "N" word once by another kid. She told me that night when she asked me to tuck her in bed. She had tears in her eyes. I had tears in my eyes.

Liina, our biological daughter, once asked me, "What does 'biracial' mean?" I told her, and then I asked her how she felt about having sisters who were black. She said, "I don't know. It's just the way the family is."

"I hate the question, 'What is it like to be in a multiracial family?' It's like being asked how I feel about living on planet Earth when I've never lived anywhere else."
—Olisa Laufer

61

I'm curious to see if all of these people who think it's fine for their kids to be friends with our children will feel differently when their children fall in love with our children of color.

PRAKASH

The best part of being a multiracial family is setting an example that it's a natural thing. Diversity is much easier to talk about when people can see it in real families like ours. It's even better when people can experience it in their own families.

OLISA

I hate the question, "What is it like to be in a multiracial family?" It's like being asked how I feel about living on planet Earth when I've never lived anywhere else.

THE LAZARE FAMILY

Louise Lazare · Aaron Lazare · Robert (28) · Karen (Robert's wife)
David (27) · Jacqueline (27) · Sarah (25) · Hien (24) · Thomas (23)
Naomi (17) · Kyle (5)

LOUISE

In our family, you have virtually every possible target for taking offense—ethnically, racially, and religiously.

We did try to live in a community that was integrated, and we supported the local introduction of busing inner-city black kids to suburban schools.

AARON

While walking with my wife, Louise, a few years ago, I asked her what she believed prompted us to adopt our eight children. In a heartbeat, she responded, "Insanity." As our discussion continued, we recollected a higher principle—that every child is entitled to be raised in a loving family. That was it. We were not attempting to make any social statement. We never sought or desired notoriety. We just kept taking children at about seventeen-month intervals until we felt too tired, too old, and too much in debt.

My mother's parents left Romania for the United States shortly after the First World War and opened a tiny fruit store in a poor, mixed black-white neighborhood in Bayonne, New Jersey. They lived in two rooms behind the store. When I visited the store, my grandfather often asked older black children from our neighborhood to keep an eye on me.

My mother often spoke to us children about the importance of racial and religious equality. In one of the most profound memories of my childhood, she entered the kitchen after returning from a shopping trip. She told me that a little black boy had tugged at her coat to get her attention. He pointed to the classic poster, "Uncle Sam Wants You!" which hung prominently in the store. He said: "Ma'am, is he my uncle too?"

After adopting Jacqueline and Sam, who are white, we decided in 1968 to

"If it comes down to just two people left in the world—a light-skinned man and a very light-skinned man—they're going to be prejudiced against the other. One person is going to say to the other, 'You're too light,' or 'You're too dark.'"
—Robert Lazare

63

adopt an African American child. We had learned that many of these children were going homeless. This was shortly before the race riots and Martin Luther King Jr.'s assassination. The adoption social worker thought we were crazy and tried to discourage us. My father was deeply concerned, and many relatives phoned and visited on his behalf to attempt to change our minds. We ignored them and did what we thought was right. Sarah, a three-month-old African American baby, came into our home.

Immediately after Sarah arrived home, in a symbolic act of generosity and forgiveness, my father gave her an Israel bond and became a devoted grandfather. Sarah's adoption was hard on our oldest daughter, Jackie, at first. She thought that our adopting an African American child meant that something was wrong with white children.

In 1970, we were ready for another child, and we received Tom, an eleven-month-old dark-skinned black boy, born to a thirteen-year-old child.

When Tom was five years old, I learned through a dream that I had undergone an important transformation regarding my own racial identity. In this dream, I painfully watched adult white people, who Tom knew and trusted, make fun of him over racial matters. In the dream, I looked in the mirror and observed that I, too, was black. When I awoke, I felt pleased that, deep in my heart, I identified with Tom.

To those of you reading this who are white, I want you to know that in suburbs known for their liberal outlook and fine schools, there is pervasive racism. The expectations for black children and the support for them is negatively influenced by their race. This may neither be conscious nor planned, but it exists. It took me a long time to come to this realization, and I am embarrassed at my naiveté. I was raised to believe that I could trust those in authority. These discriminatory practices are outrageous. Had I understood this sooner, I could have done better for my children.

I think most of the issues in this family have to do with it being a large family rather than being a multiracial family. Within the family, there were never any racial tensions. When Tom was seven years old, he was interviewed at a conference for adoptive families. The interviewer asked, "Tom, what has it been like to be raised in this family?" The interviewer probably expected Tom to make some profound comment on interracial adoption or the problems of a black child growing up in a white suburban neighborhood with white parents, or racial conflict within the family. Without much thought, Tom simply said, "Well, you never get lonely."

JACQUELINE

As the first child in my family and a white girl, I found I have had to protect my siblings all the time. Whether it be at school or in my present workplace, you constantly hear racial epithets going on around you. When I was in second grade, some kid told me that his mom said my mom was crazy for adopting black kids. He used the "N" word. I punched the little boy.

Of everyone in this family, I'm the only one who has searched out my biological mother, and she and I have a great relationship now. I've met her entire extended family, and I see how different my birth family is from my family. I don't know if I would be as open as I am if I had been raised with my birth family. But, my birth mom is so amazed and grateful that I was adopted into such a warm family. She's visited us here, and both our families are all integrated now. My father says, "Our family just keeps getting bigger and bigger."

When I first met my husband, he was prejudiced. It's just the way you're brought up. From meeting me, he's changed a lot, and now he's touched a lot of people and changed them. It all trickles down.

ROBERT

I'm Vietnamese American, but a lot of people think I'm Mexican. One of the hardest things is when you're going out with your friends and they don't know what your family is like. So when they use the "N" word, or words that insult Jewish, or Asian, or Italian people, I have to turn around and say, "Hey. I don't want to hear that. You're blasting my whole family away." A couple things have happened short of punches—basically you have to walk away or else you'd be beating up half the people in the world.

If it comes down to just two people left in the world—a light-skinned man and a very light-skinned man, they're going to be prejudiced against the other. One person is going to say to the other, "You're too light," or "You're too dark."

DAVID

I'm Robert's biological half-brother, and I'm also Vietnamese American. We were adopted together when I was eight and Robert was nine.

My roommate in the army was reading the newspaper about South Africa, and he said, "I wish I could be down there and shoot all of them blacks." I was sitting there polishing my boots, and I said, "Am I hearing this right?" I jumped down his throat. I had to live with him for the next six months, but he never said anything else like that.

The National Association of Black Social Workers made a public statement proclaiming that transracial adoption is a form of cultural genocide. They want to ban all adoptions like ours. I think that their statement is very hypocritical. After all, real cultural genocide happens all around the globe. I took an anthropology course and learned about many native tribes who are forced to move from their way of life to modern life. That's cultural genocide.

THOMAS

In our family, you get to know a bit about other kinds of people. It's not that we go out and do one cultural thing one day and something else the next day. It's just that you learn to have much more respect toward other cultures. You're more neutral. If I came from certain all-black families, I might be racist toward other people. Now, it's part of who I am to be familiar with all these cultures.

I think transracial adoption should be allowed to happen. It will stop all this whites against blacks. Well, that will always happen, but it will slow it down.

HIEN

I am Vietnamese African American, and I was adopted when I was four years old. I work with homeless women and their children who are from the inner city. I hear their views on white people and see the walls they put up. I meet many people who've never met anyone Jewish, and they make comments. I don't tell them about my family, but we discuss these issues in general terms.

SARAH

I'm a biracial African American. One of the most bothersome things about being in this multiracial family is explaining over and over again, "Yeah, we have this many kids from this country and that race," and listening over and over to people say, "Oh my God, your parents must be saints."

Even though we're very open, we still make mistakes in our family in terms of some people not understanding things. We've all gone to different places to get our educations and learned different things. So, coming back home, I'll see things like someone in the family using the term "Sambo," when referring to our dog, Sam, or to my brother Sam, who is white. It's a very derogatory term. So there are conflicts and tensions which some of us see and others don't see so quickly. I bring them up.

NAOMI

I want to go to an all-black college next year because I want to experience more black things in my life.

What I like best about my family is that everyone cares for each other.

KAREN

My family is Italian, so when they heard I was going to marry Robert many of them asked me, "Do you really know what you're doing? Your children will suffer." But now, knowing Robert, they love him.

Robert and I have a son, Kyle, who is five years old. He has a lifetime ahead, and he doesn't have a hope of being prejudiced.

THE LEIBOWITZ FAMILY

Sue Leibowitz · Maya (3)

SUE

I studied Spanish in high school and at college, and I lived in Mexico for a short time. I've also worked in inner-city areas with Hispanic people. When I decided to adopt, I decided I wanted to continue my link with Latin American people. Maya comes from Peru.

I have a network of families and friends with children from Peru and other Latin American countries. I also try to expose Maya to Peruvian culture as much as possible. The first concert I ever took her to when she was just ten months old was music from the Andes. I worried that she would cry or make noise, but she sat on my lap the whole time with her eyes glued to the musicians.

I often wonder how much Maya understands of different cultures and races. We often read a children's book that asks questions such as, "Do you look like your family?" The first time we read it, Maya said, "Nooo!" But since then, whenever we read it, she says, "Yeah." I tell her that some people say that we look alike, but that I'm not so sure we do.

At a very young age, whenever we looked at clothing catalogs, Maya pointed to children of color. If she saw someone who looked a little like her—perhaps an Asian or a Latin American child—she'd point to their photo and say, "Maya."

When Maya was two, we were getting ready to go to a multiracial family group potluck. Of all her stuffed animals, she chose to bring two bunnies—a brown one and a white one.

So far there haven't been any real problems. But I'm worried as Maya gets older that she'll get negative feedback because she looks different. All three-year-olds are pretty cute, but when she's fifteen, are people still going to think she's so beautiful and cute?

"When Maya was two, we were getting ready to go to a multiracial family group potluck. Of all her stuffed animals, she chose to bring two bunnies—a brown one and a white one."
—Sue Leibowitz

THE LUZ FAMILY

Maureen Luz · Keisha (5) · Tobias Kwame (3)

MAUREEN

My parents were in a mixed marriage—my mother was a white, New England Yankee and my father was a dark-skinned Portuguese. My mother's parents objected strongly to her marriage because they thought that my father was black. My mother was rebellious and married my father despite their objections in order to get out of her strict household. My mother was very liberal—I still don't know what influenced my mother's thinking.

When I was growing up, there were only a few black kids who went to my school. Back then, during the time of the Civil Rights marches and desegregation, the polite term for African American people was "Negro." I knew it was important to be respectful to black people because people weren't nice to them in the world. I didn't yet know the word "oppression," but I knew black people couldn't sit in the front of a bus or go to certain restaurants.

There was an African American boy who lived at the end of our street, and lots of kids teased him and pushed him around. He learned to be tough in response to that. One day, he pushed me when I was in the park, and I shoved him back. Then he hit me. I was a tomboy, and I had no problem fighting with boys, but I didn't want to fight with this kid because I didn't want him to think I didn't like him because he was black. That memory always stayed with me—that by not fighting with him, I was treating him differently because he was black.

When I told my mom that I was going to have a child with my Jamaican partner, she warned me that it would be hard. "Well, so far, life hasn't been that easy," I said, "so I'm not expecting it all of a sudden to get easy. If having a biracial child is hard, I'm ready to deal with it." By that time, I had been in relationships and friendships with many African Americans, and I had become very committed to learning about black culture. So, I felt like I was ready to take on the challenge of raising biracial children.

"Because my kids are multiracial, they have the advantage of being close to black people and white people. Most of us don't get to see the loving side of people of different races. But my kids do. Consequently, I'm hopeful that they will see the humanity in all people—regardless of color, or race, or any other label."
—Maureen Luz

73

The only time anything blatantly racist happened to me was when Keisha was a baby. I took her and a friend's black son to the fair. Some teen-age girl there assumed I was Puerto Rican, and she started screaming really horrible racist stuff at me. The cops told me I could press charges because of her discriminatory remarks and actions, but I just wanted the girl to leave. The cops escorted her out of the fairgrounds.

People usually just smile at us—my kids are pretty lovable.

My kids are black, and it's important for me that they are raised black because I think that otherwise they won't know who they are. Even though race is a social construct and not a real thing, in our society it's very real.

THE MADISON/ABAD FAMILY

Eileen Madison · Rodney Madison · Luis Abad (19)
Patricia Abad (18) · José Abad (12) · Reggie Madison (4)

EILEEN

As a family, we drive people nuts. Nobody can figure us out. I'm Puerto Rican, and I was married to a Cuban man who is the father of my first three kids. Then I married Rodney, who is African American, and we had Reggie. Reggie's the one who's really multicultural in this family because he eats everything—from grits to black beans to yellow rice.

Before I fell in love with Rodney, I couldn't see beauty in black people. I didn't even look for the beauty in black people. Here's the confession of the day—the first time Rodney kissed me, all I could see was my parents' faces. I was imagining what they would say if they saw me kissing Rodney—probably something like, "Oh my God!!!" When you are in a multiracial relationship, you start seeing beauty in all races. I feel like somebody took a blindfold off my eyes, and I started appreciating people for who they are, not because of what color they are.

My mother used to go to a social club in Puerto Rico which wouldn't accept black people. Since I married Rodney, she's changed, and she began advocating at the club. Now they let black people in. But still, with my family, Rodney has to behave twice as good as a Puerto Rican or a white man.

My son José has dirty blonde hair with super light skin. Little Reggie used to ask me, "When am I going to look like José?" Now he knows he's black, and that he's going to look like his daddy. At a local health center, the doctor asked me if I had adopted José—the doctor couldn't believe that José could be so blonde and light-skinned and still be my biological kid. I wanted to say to him, "Haven't you ever studied genetics?"

People believe that it's a compliment to say that I—or my kids—don't look Puerto Rican.

Not only are we dealing with a difference in color in our family, but we're

> "Kids become racist because of the way they are brought up. If you were brought up by a father who was a Ku Klux Klan member, you'd probably hate the black race because your father told you that blacks are bad. It's not that you decided to hate blacks. It's because you were taught. Nobody decides to be racist. People are taught to be racists."
> —José Abad

75

dealing with a difference in language. It's always in the back of my mind that I have an accent. I know that Rodney has felt embarrassed about it. Now he's okay, but with English-speaking friends in the past, oh, he would just die!

We recently tried to rent this house around here, but the landlord said he couldn't show it to us because the family who owned it were in Cape Cod. I kept calling him, and he kept saying, "They're still in Cape Cod. Call again." So, Rodney's sister called the landlord using her "white voice." He said, "Come by and see the house at three o'clock tomorrow." We are professionals and educated people, but people like that landlord smash your pride. It's like a lotus flower around here—everything's so beautiful on the outside, but on the inside . . .

Being in a family like ours, you grow so much to a point where you feel pity for the people who are not capable of seeing and getting something from all cultures. I think we are a very rich family in every way.

RODNEY

When I first met Eileen's mother, she told me the history of Puerto Rico and about how low the black people are considered there. She said that Eileen and I were facing a nightmare, and that our marriage would never work because blacks would never be accepted anywhere.

I don't know how to answer little Reggie when he asks about skin color. He has this one friend, Danny, with pale skin, blonde hair, and blue eyes. At first, Reggie asked, "When am I going to be like Danny?" That worried me. Then he asked, "When is Danny going to be like me?" I didn't worry as much. I say to Reggie, "It doesn't matter what color we are—we are just different colors like some people are taller than others." He'll learn about different cultures—he'll live it—so he'll know those differences. I have a temptation to try and explain it all to Reggie and give him a "Black-White-Puerto Rican talk," but he's still so young.

When people talk about multiracial families, they often say, "Well, there are no differences." And that's not the truth. There are differences, but the differences can be good things. I never thought for one minute that I'd ever be associated with a Puerto Rican, so being with Eileen has made me a lot less of a racist person—which we all need to be. I never dreamed that there would be lots of stuff in the Puerto Rican culture that I'd really like.

A taxi driver was telling me that a nearby town went downhill because of all the Puerto Ricans moving in. I let him go on, and then I said, "Too bad I don't have a picture of my family. My wife and children are Puerto Rican." I thought I'd give him something to think about.

Patricia recently told Eileen that she wanted me to be the one to give her away at her wedding someday. It was very special to hear that.

Reggie helped our older kids lose their prejudice toward blacks. Luis had a lot of bigotry in him. Patricia and José had some, but a lot less. However, when Reggie was born and was their brother, black became part of them in a way.

LUIS

When my mom married Rodney, I cared that he was black but I never expressed my feelings or had an argument about it. I was fourteen, and my own father was very racist. I'd visit him in Puerto Rico, and Dad would say lots of bad things about black people and how embarrassed he was that my mom had married a

black man. I personally felt embarrassed too. I was raised to be a racist because I spent most of my summers with my dad, and he was a big influence on me. In the past few years, I've grown apart from that side. I don't let my dad speak badly about Rodney anymore.

How can you not love Reggie? The best part of being in a multiracial family is this little guy.

PATRICIA

Some Puerto Rican kids tell me that I don't like Puerto Ricans because I have lots of white friends. They accuse me of being racist against my own people. That's screwed up. A Puerto Rican guy came up to me and said, "I didn't know you were Puerto Rican." He kept repeating it, and I kept saying to him, "What do you think makes someone a Puerto Rican? Just how you look?"

Sometimes when I go over to some of my white friends' houses, the parents see me as just a little lower. I can just sense it. It's weird.

I feel like I can't be racist against any people. At school, I made an effort to interact with the Cambodian students and they are pretty cool people. There are all these people in the world who look different from you, but they are so much like you. It's so strange!

JOSÉ

I like being in a multicultural family. There should be more families like mine because it's nice to have a mixture of a lot of races. People shouldn't judge people by what their skin color is, but by what their personality is—just like my mom did with Rodney. Now I have family members from Rodney's side who talk about their lives, and so I know more about what another race goes through.

My family is sort of different, and I like being different from other people because I don't want to just be a number. I want to be a different family.

I think God wanted people to be different and to understand what differences really are. If you're a different race, then you're not lower—you're just a little different. Everybody's different. Nobody's the same even within the same race.

I know of a white man who married a Chinese woman, and they adopted four children of all races. I really think it's great because they don't care about what culture or race anyone is from—they just care about what each kid is like.

Some kids try to help adopted kids a little more because they're adopted, but they don't really need to be helped. Being adopted is just the same thing as being birthed—you're being taken care of, and you're having a loving family.

Kids become racist because of the way they are brought up. If you were brought up by a father who was a Ku Klux Klan member, you'd probably hate the black race because your father told you that blacks are bad. It's not that you decided to hate blacks. It's because you were taught. Nobody decides to be racist. People are taught to be racists.

My dad has the personality of racism. He thinks he's a little better than everyone else. I don't like that. But all around, he's really a good person. I ignore the bad things he says.

When I tell kids that Rodney's my stepdad, they're all surprised. They think that such a family can't happen, so it's usually a problem for them. But some people really understand. There's another multiracial family next door, and I'm good friends with the older kid. He and I talk about multiracial families. He always says to me, "Yeah, that happens to me too."

I was talking with a friend who made a racist comment. I said, "Wait a second, I'm Puerto Rican." Then he said, "Oh my God!" I was really mad. I think he learned not to judge people by what they look like.

We moved to Chicago for a year, and my school was almost all black kids. Because I look white, the black kids there called me, "white boy." I'm not white. I'm Puerto Rican. I always tell people that I'm Puerto Rican because people don't know it by looking at me. Just because I look white doesn't mean I'm white.

I like Puerto Rican culture a lot. My aunt has parties, and we dance. On the Fourth of July, after the fireworks were over, we decided to stay out in the field by her house, and my uncle brought out his stereo. Well, I don't really know how to dance, but I try to do the Puerto Rican dances like the Merengue.

I have black friends, Puerto Rican friends, and white friends. It depends on the person. Sometimes, I might make a racist comment—because a person is so bad, I might stereotype him. But then, I realize that I said something wrong, and I try to fix that up.

In the junior high, there's one table where all the black kids sit, and all the Puerto Rican kids sit together at another table. It's really bad. I don't like that. I go with my black cousin and try to mix up the black group. They know I'm Puerto Rican, so they take me. They are a little racist about white people, but it's because of all the trouble they've gone through. So I understand it. In grammar school, it was much easier—we got to know all the kids past the stereotypes.

I think there should be special classes in school that talk about all the races so you can understand them. If you don't understand somebody, you think they are lower than you, and you don't want to know them. If you understand somebody, you know them better, and you want to be friends with them.

THE MAIOLATESI FAMILY

Kate Maiolatesi · Al Maiolatesi · Laida Rose (4)

KATE

Most people assume that Laida is our biological child because she's blonde and light-skinned like me. Actually, we adopted Laida. Her birth mother is a biracial African American woman with medium brown skin, and her birth father is white.

When I told my father that we were going to adopt a biracial child, he said, "What difference does it make? A child is a child. You can love a child whatever color it is. Who cares what race she is?"

Al and I were really excited about learning about another race and having it be an intimate part of our life. We were, honestly, a bit taken aback when Laida turned out to look so white.

Laida told Al that she saw someone who looked like our black friend Tony. Al said to Laida, "Even though you don't look like Tony, in a way you're the same as Tony too." She said, "No I'm not. He has brown skin." This whole thing is—and will continue to be—very confusing for her. When Laida looks in the mirror, she's never going to see her African American heritage reflected; and yet, I think it's so important for every child to know and understand and honor whatever racial heritage they have.

Laida went through a period when she kept saying, "I don't like black people from Africa." Al and I were worried that somebody had told her that black people were bad. Then she began saying, "I don't like those white people from Africa too." I was totally confused by that. I asked her what she was talking about, and Laida pointed to a calendar on our wall. It had a photograph of African people, some of whom had their faces painted white—they looked scary to Laida because they were dressed in ceremonial robes. We were relieved.

Because Laida looks white, people might say racist things in front of her. If she were a darker-skinned kid, people might keep themselves in check a little

"Because Laida looks white, people might say racist things in front of her. If she were a darker-skinned kid, people might keep themselves in check a little more. I wonder—as she grows up—if she will think, 'It's a good thing that I can hide my African American side.' Hopefully, she will choose to challenge these racist comments and share what she knows about both sides."

—Kate Maiolatesi

more. I wonder—as she grows up—if she will think, "It's a good thing that I can hide my African American side." Hopefully, she will choose to challenge these racist comments and share what she knows about both sides.

AL

My relatives are openly racist. When I was a little kid, they made comments about black people on the street who weren't even part of their lives! It made no sense to me. I remember a time when I was getting on the bus with my mom and an aunt. The only seat open was next to a black woman, and my mother sat down there. My aunt started to make a fuss, and my mother told her to stop. Afterward, my aunt tried to give my mother a hard time. My mother said, "I was tired. I wanted to sit down. I don't care who I sit next to."

My mom had some prejudices—we all do—but she wasn't a blatant racist. Probably, that's why I didn't develop those strong negative attitudes. But, no matter what color you are, if you are born in this country, you are prejudiced. There's no denying it. It's just a matter of degree and what you do with it once you know it's wrong.

I grew up where I had zero contact with anyone of color. Racial issues—I thought then—were not my issues, not my problem. And now they are. It's that simple.

We didn't make a conscious decision to adopt a biracial baby. We didn't even make a conscious decision to adopt a baby. Kate got the phone call about Laida, and she whispered to me, "Do we want a baby?" I said, "Yes." And she said, "Yes." And that was that. At that point, Laida was ours. There was no turning back. If it turned out that she had been purple, it wouldn't have mattered.

We want Laida to either be proud—or, at the very least, be indifferent about her heritage. I don't feel particularly proud of being Italian—it's fun sometimes, but mostly it's nothing special. It just *is*. And if she feels that way about being black, it's fine with me.

Where we live now is so different from the place I grew up. I love seeing Laida at day care and at parties—the rooms are full of Asian kids, Indian kids, white kids, and African American kids.

When I went to a family reunion recently, some guy made a nasty crack about black people but nobody said anything. I got really pissed off and confronted the man. I said, "My daughter is African American, and I don't want her hearing this kind of language, so why don't you rethink how you look at people?" Afterward I realized that I shouldn't have made it into a personal thing. Rather, I should have used it as an opportunity to educate him about racism in general. At any rate, I walked out, and when I returned later, my cousins apologized for him and told me that he was a really nice man. I said, "He's a racist—I can't get past that. How can he be a nice man if he hates?" Kate and I don't visit those relatives anymore. We don't trust them.

We went to the county fair recently and saw at least a dozen young interracial couples. I think it's absolutely healing. For every multiracial family, maybe there are a hundred people in their extended family network who suddenly have to deal with having another race in their life.

THE MATLOCK FAMILY

Delayne Matlock · Ben Matlock · Adam Matlock (7)

DELAYNE

When I was in kindergarten, my first teacher was very white, and she had blonde hair. That scared me, and I remember hiding from her. She was my image of a ghost. I got used to her, but I'll never forget the sight.

As a child, I didn't hate white people, but I hated their actions a lot. I didn't associate with them.

Ben and I met in Germany, and we spent fourteen years there. Adam was born there. In Germany, you can get sued if you make a racist remark, and many African Americans will tell you that when they go to Germany, they are well respected and not a target for racism. I didn't have any fear being with Ben and Adam until I came back to the United States. Here, racism is woven completely into our society.

I started the Harmony Choir to enlighten people through music about our ancestors, because we don't get much history in school about Africans and early African American life. With this music, we can pass our history on in a positive way. Harmony Choir performs all over the country—in churches, in schools, and even at the United Nations.

Adam can "talk black" around black people and "talk white" around white people. The only difference between Adam and a black child is that he has a white parent who is involved in the white world. But don't call Adam, "white." I don't know why, but he wants to be black. He identifies with black people. He thinks it's wonderful being black and has no problem with who he is. Once he said his dad was, "light, light, light black."

If you're going to raise a child together, it's not about which culture is the best. Both Ben and I want to help Adam fit into civilization, and we both have to work toward that. All children should be taught manners and to respect adults, other children, and themselves.

"Being biracial gives our son, Adam, a real advantage. Unlike so many people of one race, he'll never be able to form a solid opinion about folks—he's caught in two worlds. He won't always consider this an advantage, I'm sure, but, ultimately, I think he will."

—Ben Matlock

BEN

I grew up in a Christian family in a white Midwestern town, and my parents would often say, "Love thy neighbors." I didn't realize then that they didn't mean people who were different from us. But, for me, I've always been open to other people. I find difference interesting and intriguing.

When my family found out I was going to marry Delayne, they worried about what the neighbors would think of their son marrying a black woman. Once it came out into the light, it was no big deal for their neighbors, which helped my parents a lot. And after Adam was born, my parents changed instantly, because they loved him.

Being biracial gives Adam a real advantage. Unlike so many people of one race, he'll never be able to form a solid opinion about folks—he's caught in two worlds. He won't always consider this an advantage, I'm sure, but, ultimately I think he will.

THE MERCIER FAMILY

Diane Mercier · Christina (10) · Crystle (9) · Cynthia (8)

"I love my daughters. I don't see brown skin on them. I don't see white skin on them either. I just see my children. My daughters are my daughters."—Diane Mercier

DIANE

I'm French Canadian with some Canadian Indian. The father of my children is Puerto Rican. So my kids are half-and-half.

My family gave me a lot of trouble about my boyfriend. I know they didn't like him because of his color. They all said I should have my own color kids after they found out I was pregnant, but that just made me determined to have more kids.

My family accepts the kids, but not as much as I would like them to. My kids see the prejudice too.

I learn to let it go in one ear and out the other. I forgive but I don't forget. It's been a long time since my sister called me a nasty name. I still bring it up to her once in a while, but she doesn't want to hear it.

It's going to be hard for my daughters because there's a lot of prejudiced people out there, but I'll help them as much as I can. I'd fight for my daughters.

I love my daughters. I don't see brown skin on them. I don't see white skin on them either. I just see my children. My daughters are my daughters.

THE MILLER FAMILY

Lisa Miller · Jedd Miller · Elijah (10) · Jenna Hae Lee (6)

LISA

After we had Elijah, we wanted another child. I went to an adoption meeting and saw a woman carrying a Korean baby. I held the baby, looked at Jedd, and said, "This is it."

The best part of being in a multiracial family is appreciating Jenna's incredible individuality and beauty. I feel grateful that she brings elements to our family that would not exist had we not adopted her.

Jenna has been teased because she's Korean, which can make a parent feel incredibly protective. My own grandmother, whom I adore, was in the hospital. Jenna and I went to visit her and she introduced us to the nurse as, "My granddaughter Lisa and her adopted daughter, Jenna." I said, "My daughter!! My DAUGHTER." I felt incredibly upset at that moment.

We had one experience in a supermarket where a kid asked why Jenna looks the way she does. Jenna said, "I'm from Korea," and the kid made a real snide comment. I felt such a rage come up in me, and Jenna got really upset. I gave the kid a lecture on racism, which didn't seem to faze him in the least. Jenna and I went out to the car, and we talked for a really long time about how it made her feel. That night, Jenna told Elijah and Jedd what had happened. Elijah was great. He told Jenna, "That kid was wrong. He said something really nasty, and it's not true." This seemed to ease some of Jenna's pain. Elijah is very aware of racism now. We have been very lucky that we have not had any other experiences like this one.

One of the most challenging things for us is exposing Jenna to Korean culture and finding resources to keep her connected to her Korean roots. She has many books, dolls, and clothes. At the same time, we are Jewish. Jenna was converted, and she is in Hebrew school. She will become a bat mitzvah at thirteen. We practice Jewish ritual in our home.

"I've had both a biological child and an adopted child. As soon as Jenna was handed to me at the airport, it was no different from when I held my son for the first time after his birth. It was incredible."
—Lisa Miller

I think Jenna looks like me—a lot, except for the shape of her eyes.

I've had both a biological child and an adopted child. As soon as Jenna was handed to me at the airport, it was no different from when I held my son for the first time after his birth. It was incredible.

JEDD

I can literally remember when I was sixteen knowing that I wanted to have some kind of international family. I don't even know why exactly. It just seemed like a natural thing.

When we adopted Jenna, I thought that there's just this basic unity of all people. But there's a lot of real big differences too. I'd like for her to know all her parts real clearly, so we will need to keep her connected to Korean culture. We're going to take Elijah to Israel for his bar mitzvah when he's thirteen, and I'd like to take Jenna to Korea when she's a teen-ager.

We don't think on a daily basis, "Oh, our multicultural family . . ." Rather it is simply "our family." We have enormous love. We have struggles and challenges like any family. Yes, there are struggles that are particular to a multiracial family, but it makes you work with differences in a very conscious and compassionate way.

We call ourselves "Boo-Jews"—Buddhist Jews. That's why Jenna was such a perfect fit. Lisa and I felt a clear affinity with Asian kids.

ELIJAH

I don't treat Jenna any different than if she was a biological sister. I want people to know that they shouldn't look at us as any different from any other family.

JENNA

Being in a multiracial family is not different than being in any other family!

THE MUSANTE/BARTMON FAMILY

Lisa Musante · Fred Bartmon · Nicholas (8) · Peter (5) · Tamaia (2)

LISA

After the boys were in school, I really wanted another child. I had always wanted to adopt a child, and through our research, we found that there were more children of color needing families. After examining our own lives and our community, we felt that the necessary resources were within us and available to us to provide a child of color with what she needed to develop a strong racial identity and high self-esteem. Tamaia came into our lives when she was two years old from the island of Saint Lucia.

Before Fred and I adopted Tamaia, my mother expressed concern for her grandsons. She asked, "What's this going to be like for the boys? They're going to come face-to-face with racism and discrimination." My feeling was—and is even stronger now—that it's going to be an important experience for my sons. They are going to grow up knowing someone of another race intimately. Because of this, they will have an awareness of the obstacles Tamaia has to face simply because of her race.

Before we adopted Tamaia, I asked some African American friends how they felt about white families adopting black children. Ideally, they said, every child should be raised by a family of the same race. But, the most important thing—according to these friends—was for every child to have a loving family of their own.

I have to admit that there are times when I wonder if I can be an adequate role model for Tamaia. And sometimes, I wonder what members of the black community think when they see Tamaia with her white family, but so far the response has been very positive. Two black women, whom I didn't know, have asked for my phone number so that we can get our kids together to play.

I was at the playground with Tamaia recently. A little African American boy was totally confused by us after he heard Tamaia calling me "Mommy." He said,

> *"Before we adopted Tamaia, I asked some African American friends how they felt about white families adopting black children. Ideally, they said, every child should be raised by a family of the same race. But, the most important thing—according to these friends—was for every child to have a loving family of their own."*
>
> —Lisa Musante

"You can't be her mommy." I said, "Yes, I am." Then he asked me, "Is her daddy black?" I said, "No," and then I explained that we had adopted Tamaia.

Our whole family has changed in terms of sensitivity to racial issues. Now, Nicholas's drawings often include people of different colors playing together. He also had a very strong emotional reaction to his classroom's study of Rosa Parks and the busing boycott. And Peter has become more aware of differences in skin color among his friends and comments upon these differences in a matter-of-fact way.

FRED

My parents are extremely humane, liberal people who made me very conscious about racism at an early age. They taught me to accept people of all races. Ironically, we lived in an affluent white suburb where we only had contact with rich white people. When I went away to college, it took me a few years to acclimate myself to a world other than the very homogeneous, wealthy place I had grown up in.

My brother was adopted. He was born with a cleft lip, and none of the other couples who were ahead of my parents on the adoption agency waiting list wanted him. Finally, the agency asked my parents if they wanted him and they said, "Of course we do." They didn't even go down and look at him. That's another example of how I was raised.

I'm oblivious to what people think about me and about our family—and I don't worry about any future problems. Tamaia's just this great little girl who is part of our family. I'm sure that things will hit us, and we'll deal with them—but it's not as if I'm preparing myself in some special way for Tamaia. I think we're going to be competent if problems come up.

THE NWOKOYE FAMILY

Anne Nwokoye · Nkiruka Ramona (21) · Ifeoma Justina (18)
Ekene Annielaurie (15)

ANNE

My mother raised all of her kids in a multiracial, multicultural environment in Washington, D.C. I knew about racism as a kid, but I didn't relate it to myself.

When I was going to get married, my future husband wrote a letter to my mother. In it, he told her his career plans, and said that he wanted me to be by his side. My mother didn't mention getting the letter, so finally I asked her about it. She said, "Oh, yes, it was very nice, but he forgot to say anything about his being black." And I said, "Well, Nigerians wouldn't think of saying that." To Nigerians, race just isn't such a big issue.

For my wedding, my mother decided she would put an announcement in the *New York Times* and she printed the invitations at Tiffany's. I said, "Mother, I don't want all this." I asked her why she was doing that, as she had renounced upper-class values when she had gotten married. She thought about it and said, "I must be trying to make *it* okay, and I don't need to do it this way." She trashed all the plans and tore the invitations up.

My grandmother was very prejudiced. She was raised in the West Indies in the super waspy, white, English upper-class and her family had descendants of slaves as servants. I had dated black men and it wasn't okay with Granny, so I didn't tell her that I was going to be married until two months before the wedding. She just looked at me and said, "Is he black?" And I said, "Yeah." "Very black?" she asked. "Yeah," I replied. After a long pause, she said, "Well, if it makes you happy to marry him, then it makes me happy."

Later on, my mother told me that when Granny was a young woman she had fallen in love with a man who was "passing for white." She wanted to marry him, but when her family found out that one of his great-grandparents was black, the wedding was called off, and she was devastated. So, perhaps she was saying to me, "Go for it, girl!"

"My mother told me that I have a choice of how I want to live my life. I can live anywhere in the world. I can do whatever I want to do. I don't have to be in black America or in white America. I just want to create my own life. I can just be me."
—Ekene Nwokoye

After my husband and I separated in Nigeria, I returned to the United States with our daughters. I overheard a man speaking a Nigerian language in a restaurant, and I went up to him. He took me to meet the Ibo families who live nearby, and I joined a Nigerian organization. The people in the Nigerian community treat us like we're family.

NKIRUKA

White people normally don't see people like me and my sisters as multiracial. We're not thought of as "half," we're definitely seen as black—and that can be positive or negative. If they find out we're biracial, they're surprised, but it quickly leaves their mind. It's really hard to represent both sides because most people don't see the white side.

I left Nigeria when I was ten, and most of my childhood memories are there. I still speak the language, and I went back to visit my father last summer. I'd like to go to Nigeria for a whole year because I want to be able to function as an adult in the Ibo culture. I want to hold my own and not feel like a visitor. I think I can do that.

Nigerians have a different attitude toward interracial families than do African Americans. Nigerians have not been oppressed as directly by white people as the black people in America have been. So while I was growing up in Nigeria, being biracial was never an issue for me. People took notice of our lighter skin color, but there was no value attached to it.

Coming to America was hard for me. I was immediately perceived as black, and I had to learn what it means to be black in America. It was a new thing and a very painful, psychologically twisted thing. I just had to come to terms with it. In puberty, the popularity thing was so important and because I was one out of a few black kids, I could never have been popular. And before that, I was considered so cute in Nigeria!

I've been remembering how I consciously used to want to be white. I'd look in the mirror and think, "Why can't I look more white?" I would try to figure out what about my features could possibly be mistaken for white. I never had that desire in my life until I moved to America.

I never announce to people that I'm mixed unless it's something I'm talking about for a reason. I'm not trying to push it out of my consciousness. That's what I am, and I accept it. It's not a problem for me now, but I've gone through a lot because of it.

I can't deny that being light-skinned and being very familiar with white culture has helped me in school and at job interviews. And a lot of black guys have fallen into the whole ideal of light-skinned black women, so it has probably helped me get more dates too. All of this causes resentment in darker-skinned black people. I don't blame them.

One of the biggest underlying reasons why my sisters and I are very concerned with what black people think of us is because the entire society views us as black. We don't really have the option of going into the white world.

I'll marry whomever I fall in love with, but I think it's really hard dealing with being biracial. It sounds so awful, but if I married a white man, my kids would be so light that they'd probably have a very hard time. If I did marry a white man, I don't know where I'd raise our kids, but I cringe to think of raising them in America.

Being biracial is one of those things that makes people say, "It seems like a horrible burden at first, but it could turn out to be a gift." I do appreciate that my mother is white. Because of her, I don't feel completely alienated from a whole segment of the human race. I know my mother and my mother's family, and I totally respect them and love them, so I know that not all white people are bad. I feel much more open-minded.

Being biracial in America, your life could go so many different ways. It could have been all messed up. To me, it's the grace of God that we all came out so well.

EKENE

When I was in third grade, I had an experience that has lasted with me to this day. My mother had just given me an Afro haircut, which was a new style for me. I was very, very sensitive as a child anyway, but coming into class with this kind of haircut was a huge step for me, and I was very insecure about it. I can still remember this kid who laughed and pointed at me and made fun of my hair. Inside, I felt this darkness enveloping me. It was like, "Oh no, I've made a grave mistake. This is not right. I'm different. Why did I ever do this?"

I would know that kid's face if I saw it in fifty years because his image—the way his eyes looked, the way his face looked—is imprinted in my head forever. I absorbed that feeling of shame, and it stayed with me throughout my life. It has taken me years to be able to feel free with my hair, to feel free with the way I look, and to be 100 percent confident since then. I will never forget that experience.

There was pressure not to have white friends at school, but I did anyway. I had a serious complex about that for a while. Black Americans have their anger and their oppression and all that pain, and the ones I knew wanted me to understand and carry the pain with me too. I was told by some black friend that if you're really black, you've got to be angry all of the time, and you've got to make fun of white people. You have to hold these beliefs.

I remember one time an African American friend of mine was talking about Duke Ellington, and I didn't even know who he was. My friend was shocked. People expect that since you are black, you must know certain things. You must be "down." But I didn't grow up with that stuff, so the pressure to know all those things was confusing.

My mother told me that I have a choice of how I want to live my life. I can live anywhere in the world. I can do whatever I want to do. I just want to create my life. I don't have to be in black America or white America. I can just be me.

IFEOMA

I remember all of us girls running around the supermarket when we were little. People quickly figured out that Anne was our mom. If we went out with her now, I wonder if anyone would make that connection.

It's been so hard to try and fit in with black Americans when you're not black American. I'm Nigerian and American, and there's such a cultural difference between a West African and a black American. If we were to truly live up to who we are, we would identify more fully with our Nigerian side. That was very difficult when I was younger, so I almost trained myself to be a black American. I bought magazines, learned to talk a certain way, went to certain parties. It was never really me.

A lot of times in the black community, you are made to feel ashamed of being mixed. I know some people who would never ever admit to being biracial, and yet they're the ones who claim they are the most "black." If you do talk about being biracial, some black people might assume that you're bragging and saying that you're better than them.

The mixed kids with light hair and blue eyes have the hardest time with it. They have to prove they're black twice as hard as anyone else.

I'm definitely judged more harshly by black people than I am by white people. I've been called an "Oreo" by black people. If it's known that you're mixed, you can be written off as not being dedicated to helping the black community—as not really being black.

Because I had white friends at my school, the black kids assumed I was a snob. "Ify thinks she's too good for us," they would say. I'd look at the black kids and think, "If they don't want to accept me, why should I turn to them?" So, I just stayed with my white friends. This separation finally broke down during my senior year in high school.

One white teacher at my school was overheard saying, "Well, Ify doesn't really count as a minority. She's not really black." I didn't know how to take this, how it was supposed to make me feel. Even some of the white kids have said to me, "Ify, I don't think of you as *different*." I've made more effort to try, when people say such ignorant things around me, to raise their consciousness.

If I had just grown up in a black community, I would be so sheltered and I would have such a narrow vision of things. I feel so enlightened in a way having all these sides. I feel like I know a lot about the black community and the white community, and I feel so privileged that I can have all this knowledge. You do get strength.

I've definitely come to terms with my identity and feel pretty comfortable. I always think how lucky I am—considering all the things we've had to go through—that I have my sanity. It's disproved the idea that you have to be mixed up if you are biracial.

THE O'NEILL/HOLLAND FAMILY

Susan O'Neill · George Holland · Amanda (7) · Zachary (3)

SUSAN

George and I decided to adopt because I was infertile, and I wanted to have a baby. George already had an adopted African American daughter, Chrissy, from his first marriage. We thought if we adopted black kids, it would be a plus for them to have someone in the family already who was adopted and black. For myself, I felt a connection to African American culture and heritage from things I had studied. When I was in college, I was deeply involved in the Civil Rights movement.

When Mandy was younger, she used to talk about wanting to be like me and have my color skin. In response to that, I used to talk about how I wanted to be like her, and we discussed the idea of trading. That issue hasn't come up again, and it hasn't surfaced yet with Zack.

Mandy told me, "You know, I'm really glad I'm not the only brown one in my class. My friend Caroline has so many kids that are like her, and I have just one." So, when the teachers were making their class lists for the next year, I found out that they were going to separate Mandy and her African American friend into different classrooms. When I told the teachers that Mandy really liked having the other black child with her, they kept them together.

The mixed race of our family has made me really appreciate the experience of people who are different in our world and what it must be like for them to live in a white culture.

Black women have offered to help me with my children's hair. Nobody has ever said anything negative to us.

In the past few years, I've had college students from Africa as our baby sitters. Each one is a very different person from a very different cultural background. I like having these students feel like part of our family on a regular basis, and I feel

"When I talk about adoption, I tell people that I can't imagine Mandy or Zack feeling any more mine than if they came out of my body. They come out of your soul, and it's just an incredible experience."
—Susan O'Neill

lucky that they can bring something of Africa to our children's experience.

When I talk about adoption, I tell people that I can't imagine Mandy or Zack feeling any more mine than if they came out of my body. They come out of your soul, and it's just an incredible experience.

GEORGE

In my first marriage, I already had two biological white children before we adopted Chrissy, who is black. My parents had a strong reaction to the idea of us adopting a black child, but as soon as they met her, they fell in love with her. They've given Chrissy, Mandy, and Zack as much as they've given to any of their other grandchildren. It's been amazing to see that, when put in this situation, they do all the nice things that good grandparents do.

When Chrissy was a kid and she got mad at me and her mom, she'd sometimes say, "I'm going to see my black parents. Maybe they'll understand me better than you." It was fluff, so it didn't get to me that much.

At college, Chrissy wants to connect much more with people of her own race, and she's currently dating someone from Barbados. Gillian, my twenty-four-year old white daughter, mostly dates black guys too.

One thing that strikes me sometimes when I look at my kids is that the adopted ones feel as much my kids as my biological ones do, which goes against what most people think. I go back to the same old thing—a sperm and an egg don't make a parent. What makes a parent is getting up at night and taking care of a kid.

I get very angry at the black social workers' organization not wanting whites to bring up black kids. Part of me wants to say, "I've just got a family here, folks, so bug off. I'm going to raise Mandy and Zack just like I raised my three other kids before, and I don't want to deal with all this other stuff."

THE PICKRON FAMILY

Lisa Pickron · Carlton Pickron · Charisse Burgundy (8) · Marita Joy (5)

LISA

I grew up in a very white city—there was only one black student in the entire high school. I think my parents did try to bring us up to believe that everybody is created equal, at least in theory. I don't think they were bothered much by the idea of interracial marriage in general; however, when it came to their daughter, that was a different story.

I wrote to my mom during my freshman year at college and told her I was dating a black guy. I explained that he was going away at the end of the summer, so probably nothing would happen. She wrote me back and said, "That's so nice. We've always raised you to believe that we're all created equal." But, when I came home later on, and it became clear to my mom that my relationship with Carlton had become serious, she nearly hit the roof. She felt that I had deceived her. It was okay to date him, but not to marry him.

My mother is half French Canadian and half English. My mother's mom didn't want my mother to marry my father because she thought that their children would be too dark because he's Italian. And my father had blue eyes and fair skin—he wasn't dark at all! In spite of going through that, my mother saw marrying a black man in a different light.

The big thing my parents kept saying to me about my decision to marry Carlton was, "What about the children? The children are going to be hurt, and then you're going to feel hurt." But I was determined, with or without my parents' approval, that I was going to marry him. They have long since welcomed Carlton as part of the family, and they love our children as dearly as their other grandchildren.

When we applied for mortgages, I called a bank and this guy was so enthusiastic. I told him about our jobs and our income. "Come on in," he urged us over

"Somebody asked my daughter, 'Why is your daddy black and your mommy white?' She answered, 'Because that's what they are.'"
—Carlton Pickron

the phone, but he changed his tune when he saw us. He sent us away with just a quick good-bye.

One time, a four-year-old girl told Charisse that black girls couldn't be princesses because black girls aren't pretty. Strangely, that girl's parents are a liberal white and Latino mixed couple. Obviously kids can get this racist stuff from other places than their own parents.

Kids get confused sometimes when they see our family. They'll say to Charisse and Marita, "Is that your mother?" Or adults will ask me, "Are those kids yours?" It doesn't really bother me. Even my seven-year-old nephew had this perception that I must be black because I'm married to Carlton. He just couldn't figure it out.

When Charisse was about to go to first grade she said, "Mommy, will there be anyone else with curly hair like me?" I think she was really asking, "Will there be other black children?" Sometimes she says, "I wish I had straight hair like yours, Mommy," even though everyone compliments her on her hair. I think she realizes that she's different from the majority of people where we live.

Sometimes Marita will ask, "Is my skin color this shade or closer to that shade?" There's no value judgment. She's just comparing.

CARLTON

Before I went away to college at a predominantly white school, this black guy told me, "Well, it's all right to go there and be friends with them, but don't bring any of them home." He was talking about white women. My mother never said anything one way or the other. She had always wanted me to go to good schools, and that always meant being bused to the white schools. My mother exposed me to white people all of my life.

My mom loves Lisa, loves the kids, and loves the fact of us together working and doing what we do. I know she's quite proud of our accomplishments as a family, and it's clear she's proud that I'm still with Lisa and the kids, because my father left her when I was only two.

Lisa and I got married in a Catholic church because Lisa is Catholic. My uncle was a Baptist minister, and he assisted in our wedding service. According to Lisa's mother, people are still talking about that wedding ceremony today.

For me, it's important that our girls have books, dolls, and games that reflect diversity. I don't want them to have all black and white dolls. I want them to have a variety of dolls, and I want them to understand that all people are valuable and important. I also want them to understand the realities of our society and what's out there.

Yes, Mommy and Daddy gave them a lifelong challenge. Charisse and Marita will always have to explain who they are to other people.

When the girls get to the point of filling out applications or forms that ask about race, I hope there will be a multiracial category. If not, I hope they will always mark down both black and white. That's very important to me because they are not one over the other.

Somebody asked Charisse, "Why is your daddy black and your mommy white?" She answered, "Because that's what they are."

CHARISSE

Family is different people from different places with different heritages who love each other and look out for each other.

For me, the best part of being in my family is that my parents love me.

I think that someone once said that I was different, or that I wasn't good because I'm different. But I don't remember exactly. I wouldn't want to be in a different family than mine.

I like being in a multiracial family. I think it's better, from my point of view, to be in a multiracial family. You learn more about your ancestors, so you might know more than other kids do about some things. I'm interested in my ancestry. I do African dance.

MARITA

My mom knows some ways to do things and my dad knows other ways to do things, so I'll know two ways to do things.

I like to eat Italian food, macaroni and cheese, and sweet potato pie. I celebrate Kwanzaa, and I like to do African dance.

I like my family because my mom knows more about bugs and my dad knows more about African cloth.

THE RHODES FAMILY

Penny Rhodes · Irv Rhodes · Caelah (23) · Lauren (16)

PENNY

I grew up in a Jewish neighborhood in a northeastern city, and the neighborhoods were, and still are, very segregated. We didn't have any interactions with non-Jewish kids. What prepared me for an interracial relationship is Judaism itself—the fact that Jews understand persecution and can generalize past their own experience to another group's experiences. There are a lot of intermarriages between Jewish women and black men.

My mother was upset when I told her I was going to marry Irv. It was my second marriage, and I had a white daughter, Caelah, already. My mother was afraid more than anything for the impact on Caelah's life, and, if Irv and I had children, on their lives.

Another relative of mine walked in the door, saw Irv, walked out, and didn't want to speak to me again. It was because Irv was black, not because Irv wasn't Jewish.

When a white person marries someone black, they cease to be the "regular" white person they were before. They become a witness to institutional racism. People are very comfortable being racist when they think nobody around is going to tell. So, when you make a commitment through marriage or by adoption to love a person of color, you're also agreeing to take on the impact of racism too—particularly when you raise a kid. If you have a nice white child, you can expect the child to be successful on her own merits and reap the benefits of the culture. With a child of color, it just isn't that simple.

IRV

I grew up in a small town in Pennsylvania that was racially mixed, and I had black friends and white friends. Even though there was still racial separation all

"If you see an interracial couple— either gay or straight —there's a reason for it. Love hit them with an arrow, and they fell in love. It's just going to happen. Love is blind."
—Lauren Rhodes

over the country, there was a strong sense of community in our town because everyone was literally in the same position—all the fathers were coal miners. It's harder to be a racist when everyone's poor and struggling together.

My marriage with Penny has had a broad impact on people in my family, on friends of our kids, and especially on white friends of ours whose kids date black kids. Obviously, it's made it a lot easier for them to deal with that kind of situation. It's something that's not strange, not foreign—Penny and I are like guideposts. If their child goes out with a black kid, they know that lightning is not going to strike when they walk out the door.

Our marriage had an especially strong impact on my white stepdaughter, Caelah. At a young age, whenever she was asked to put down her race on school forms, Caelah checked, "Other."

Obviously, when we choose to go to certain parts of the country, we know that we're going to be stared at. It doesn't mean that we have to react—it's someone else's problem, not our problem. However, I'm always going to be very aware of how people perceive us. It's always going to be in the foreground because I've been raised as a black person in an essentially racist society. It's a part of me.

In a lot of ways, an interracial relationship is no different than a same race relationship. Our lives are filled with all kinds of perils and hazards, happiness and sadness, and goodness and badness. It's no different.

CAELAH

People have always asked me whether it was weird to grow up in a multiracial family. I've always answered, "It's my family, and it's all I've ever known. I have never thought of it as different or strange."

LAUREN

Kids in kindergarten asked me, "How come your father is black and your mother is white?" It shocked me at first. I had no clue that there was actually a big problem with it because my parents hadn't told me that it was unusual. It was terrible explaining it over and over again. But by third grade, everybody got used to it, and more biracial kids came to my elementary school.

I had problems with my identity for a while. When we were filling out forms in third grade, I checked the category "Black." Then in sixth grade, I told all the biracial kids to check the box marked "Other," because we weren't black and we weren't white.

When I was younger, my mom and I were in Atlanta visiting the Ebenezer Baptist Church where Martin Luther King preached. A black man saw us and called out, "Look, there's a white woman with a black child!"

When I went to junior high, the black kids, for some odd reason, all chose to sit together. And if I didn't always sit with them, then they thought I wasn't "really black" or there was something racist in my mind. They thought I wanted to be white, or Asian, or something else, but that I didn't want to be black.

Most of the time people say that biracial kids are black because their father or mother is black. I say, "My mom's white. Does that make me white?" They say, "No. If you have a little bit of black blood in you, then you're black."

Once I was telling a black friend about a guy I knew, and my friend asked me, "Is he black?" And I said, "No, he's biracial." My friend thought the word "biracial" was a very snobby term. She said, "He's black." And I thought, "No! He's not black. For one thing, he's not even black on the outside. He doesn't even look black. He has a black father and a white mother—so he's biracial, and you've got to deal with it." But to her, he was black. To me, it's disgusting that people use terms that people in the slave days did. To slave owners, if you had any black blood, you were black. The fact that black people are using these terms now is completely ridiculous to me. It's ironic.

Being biracial makes me see everyone's culture in a completely different way than I would have if I was just black or white. I see racism differently because I have two points of view. So being biracial makes things a bit better for me. It's very hard for me to generalize about people, and if I do, I'm kind of shocked at myself.

There was an article in *Time* magazine that said by the year 2030 there will be many more families like ours, and it won't be such a big deal. Nobody's pure anyway, so why should anyone give a care about this? Even most black kids look back at their family history and say, "Oh, there was a white slave owner back there."

If you see an interracial couple—either gay or straight—there's a reason for it. Love hit them with an arrow, and they fell in love. It's just going to happen. Love is blind.

THE ROSS-WALCOTT FAMILY

Mharia Ross-Walcott · Albert Ross-Walcott · Oya Kalimba (5) · Ekiti Bertha (3)

MHARIA

As a child, I felt the crisis of racial injustice in Washington, D.C., deeply and acutely in my bones. I felt the power of Dr. Martin Luther King's movement, the Civil Rights marches, Bobby Kennedy, the flower-power people—all of it.

When it came to choosing a partner who is both black and not American, the response from my family was varied, tentative, and somewhat distant for a while. Upon learning of my pregnancy with Oya, I was prepared for total rejection from some of my family. It was a spiritual affirmation to feel love overcome their fear of the unknown.

Albert and I have chosen to focus on building community and family with our friends, whose support is vital in our process of empowerment. The geographic distance from our families allows Albert and me the psychic space to cultivate our style as a family quite freely.

I believe my children will learn to be who they are and find their place in the larger culture. I am not saying it will be easy. I guess it is their gift to have both a father and a mother committed to parenting them, so they can directly draw from our cultural riches.

Albert and I confront our cultural differences daily in our relationship. It is faith and vision that give us the power to overcome the little worries. I give thanks that there is so much that we agree on—how to raise our children, how we keep our home, how important love and healing are. He is a great strength in my life, a teacher and a friend and a husband. I like having him for a partner. I feel that our statement is one that speaks for itself.

I believe we are changing history with the power of our conviction that this world is one planet with many forms and expressions of life. There is but one human race—we all have the same essential needs. Our greatest challenge is to preserve our lives and all of creation, to cultivate enough respect to heal the wounds of history.

"I am Oya. Sometimes when my skin is in the bathtub, I get little wrinkles from the water. My skin is light brown. When I'm in the sun a lot, my skin gets to be dark brown."
—Oya Kalimba Ross-Walcott

My greatest hope is in the potential of ourselves and our children—each one of us has a gift to give.

ALBERT

We cannot know the future of our kids. Now when they are little, we can teach them what we know, but we cannot see with our minds their future. We can set a foundation for them, but we cannot express for them. They will grow up and express themselves. When they are eighteen, they will have a mind of their own.

I'm going to prepare my kids for the world. First they need to know who they are—of mixed race, black and white. When they get older they will search their minds and the world out there and find their own identities. We are going to teach our kids that love is in every race—it is for them to find where love is in the world. I can only teach them about the world and what is out there so they can be aware of the craziness in the world.

I am coming from the culture of RastaFarI, deep down in Jamaica. A lot of sufferation, tribulation, and botheration give I enough strength to know who I is. I am here to show the world who I is and to teach my American wife and kids part of my culture, which is a strong and proud culture.

I don't know how people think about me—flashing my dreadlocks, walking with my family around town. They look at me with scorn—I can see it in their eyes, telling me with their eyes—what am I doing around here? Like I don't belong to this part of the world. Still—it is they who brought I here from Africa, on the slave ships. I walk proud with a positive vibration every day. I don't care what people think. I am living my life, because this is my life to live. Jah give I this life to live.

My relationship with Mharia is Love. Love put us together, and love will forever rule.

OYA KALIMBA

I am Oya. Sometimes when my skin is in the bathtub I get little wrinkles from the water. My skin is light brown. When I'm in the sun a lot, my skin gets to be dark brown. I wear dreadlocks because I am Jamaican. My dad has lots of dreadlocks. My sister has a little bit—some in the back but not in the front. My mom has dreadlocks too.

Our family is Rasta. We have jobs. We each have different jobs in our home because we need to take care of it and keep it nice. We like to go to California and Jamaica to visit our family and relatives. What makes us different is our natty dread hair, and we like it. Our hair is beautiful. We think Rasta is very good. We love Rasta.

EKITI BERTHA

In our family, we're Jamaican and we're American. We've got lots of friends. We have lots of treats. Mom and Dad take care of us and they love us. We have rules. We don't say, "Shut up" or "Stupid." We don't go in the street. We're RastaFarI and that means we know how to love and care. Sometimes we get mad and have to use words to work it out. We like to drum and sing songs and dance.

THE SANTIAGO WELCH FAMILY

Enid Santiago Welch · Margareta (13) · Duane (10)

ENID

I grew up in Puerto Rico until I was five. Then my family moved to Harlem where we lived in a housing project with Puerto Ricans and African Americans. Even there, my social life was completely Puerto Rican—I spoke Spanish every day.

I was nineteen when I met my husband, an African American. My mother didn't want me to marry a black man even though she didn't know him. However, she didn't give me a lot of hassle because I had always been a good kid with a good head on my shoulders. She trusted me. We married, and we had Margareta. We broke up before Duane was born.

Margareta's the darkest one of all my mother's grandchildren. My mother accepts her and loves her dearly, but my mother and the rest of my family always have to make the point that Margareta's the dark one. They say, "Oh, she's so cute, *but* she's dark." Sometimes I'd like to say to all of them, "Well, it's too bad that you're all so cute, *but* so dumb!"

Even back in biblical times, white things were considered to be pure—like the snow and the angels. That concept is something that is embedded in all of us.

I've always treated people for their individuality, for who they are, for what they are about, for their essence.

I've experienced racism, like people who apologize each time they say the word "black." One of my neighbors in this housing project told me straight out that she doesn't like Puerto Ricans. I do think it's great that she's able to say that because at least she's being honest and not trying to hide her racism.

When my kids and I first moved in here, my neighbors wouldn't talk to me, so I'd just knock on their doors and say, "Can you tell me when trash day is?" They saw that I liked to keep my garden nice, and pretty soon they were inviting me over to dinner. People treat me the way I treat them.

"I love being black and Puerto Rican. I used to feel hurt when people made fun of me. But now I don't care what people think of me because I'm me, and I can't change."
—Margareta Welch

I've had many white friends who told me that they've changed since they've gotten to know me and my kids. One friend said she had to really search her soul. Even though she had told her kids not to be prejudiced, when her daughter brought a Spanish boy to their house, she was really upset. Her daughter said, "Well, Mom, you told us not to be prejudiced." She decided that she wasn't going to be prejudiced. I feel that people have to do that—to make a decision.

I feel sad when I see people judging you because of your color. But I also have friends who say, "Enid, I don't see your color." What? Are they seeing me as a white person? I don't take it as a compliment. It's like telling somebody who is in a wheelchair, "I don't see your wheelchair." It's a bunch of crap. Each person has a color. Why not just accept the color of the person?

MARGARETA

I love being black and Puerto Rican. I used to feel hurt when people made fun of me. Now I don't care what people think of me because I'm me, and I can't change. If people don't like me for who I am, then they shouldn't bother wanting to be my friend. My self-esteem went up and that's how I started to like myself more. Now, if people make fun of my color, I just walk away.

A kid in my fifth-grade class called me the "N" word and I kicked him and punched him. At one time, I got so sick of people calling me names that I wanted to commit suicide. That was stupid of me.

It's better that I'm a person of color, or should I say black, because I don't have to get a tan. Everybody's always saying, "I need a tan." And look at me. I don't have to get one.

I feel really bad for Duane now because he's going through all the name-calling and stuff that I used to go through and he comes home crying. Obviously, it does hurt being called nasty names like "dirty Puerto Rican." But he has to learn to shake it off. I say, "Duane, you can't let ignorant people put you down. If they are going to make fun of your color, you're going to have to learn to ignore it." Most of the time I'm able to stop him from crying, but I hate seeing him go through it.

THE SBAR FAMILY

Freda Sbar · Alannah (2)

FREDA

The week after I adopted Alannah, I was taking a walk with her in a baby carrier on my chest. Two women walked by, glanced at her, and one said, "Look at the puppy." I stopped dead in my tracks. I said, "She's not a puppy!" But the women continued to talk about her as if she were a dog. This was my very first experience of racism with my child. Where I live now, people seem to be more accepting of diversity, but every once in a while we get a terrible look from someone. Alannah doesn't notice it yet.

For black children in need of homes, clearly the first choice is for them to go into a black family's home, but it is just not possible for all of the black children waiting for placement. I feel very strongly about children needing to be loved and nurtured. No child should have to languish in an institutional setting or be bounced from foster home to foster home because an agency disapproves of transracial adoption.

I never cared if I had a black child, a white child, a purple child, or a chartreuse child. Loving someone of a different race was not an issue for me. But waiting to adopt Alannah, I suddenly realized that I was going to have to deal with my parents about this difference. My family has had to deal with a lot of differences before—they considered my being a lesbian a tragedy. Ultimately I decided that they would either accept my child or not. If not, then I would simply not have contact with them.

When I first brought Alannah home, my parents didn't call me. When I finally called them, they asked minimal questions like, "Is she okay?" They were not excited. But when I went to visit them in Florida with the baby, it all changed. Now she is "their baby." My mother wants to take her to Disney World for her second birthday. It may be a little much for my mother, but Alannah will love it.

Alannah was standing in front of an opening to a tunnel of tires at a play-

> *"I never cared if I had a black child, a white child, a purple child, or a chartreuse child. Loving someone of a different race was not an issue for me."*
> —Freda Sbar

ground. A five-year-old white boy wanted to go in through that opening, despite the fact that there were many other ways to get in that were not blocked. He yelled to his mother, "There's a black kid in my way." The mother said, "Just say, 'Excuse me.'" He refused. Finally, I said to the boy, "Maybe there's a white kid in her way," and I suggested again that he say, "Excuse me." He did. Alannah let him by, and they began to play together.

I believe that being a lesbian gives me a unique perspective on oppression. Unfortunately, I don't think that society is going to make life for the black daughter of a white Jewish lesbian mother easy, but I am confident in my strength and intelligence and that of my daughter. I also believe in the strength of our family love. I know that Alannah will be a good and loving woman.

A white man who had raised two children of color told me, "Once you have a black child, you have to consider yourself black." I'm not comfortable with that statement; it may be racist in itself. But being Alannah's mom has made me look more closely at how people treat one another.

I grew up in a white, Jewish family. There was a time when I very much rejected that identity and was in conflict with my parents. I don't expect that it will be any different for Alannah. She will likely experience anger over our differences, but I honestly believe that she will learn and grow and feel the love most of all.

THE SHEGONEE FAMILY

Dawn Lindhoff-Shegonee · Art Shegonee · Maral Shegonee (9)

DAWN

I was married to a man who was part Native American, and we had Maral. After I was divorced, I met Art at a meeting about treaty rights and other Indian issues.

When I was young, I read the Classic comic book of *Hiawatha* by Longfellow. Hiawatha was a peaceful Indian, and the story was about the spirits of the animals and of the Indians. I had no trouble with Hiawatha talking to Grandmother Moon. It just made sense to me. But I never imagined that I would marry someone who was Native American. I didn't plan that.

Art and I were married by an African American minister who is known as the Martin Luther King Jr. of our city. It was definitely a cross-cultural event! We had a Christian marriage with the ring and exchange of words, and we also had a pipe ceremony honoring the four directions, which acknowledges the Native American prophecy that the people of the world will someday come together.

I wore a white wedding dress decorated with ribbons of different colors because a lot of Native Americans use ribbons. We did the reception as a potluck, so everyone from all different cultures brought all kinds of food. It was an international kind of wedding reception. The food went so fast, Art and I didn't get any.

White people are looked at by Native Americans as very dumb because they are destroying the planet. And white people often stereotype Native Americans as drunk and dumb.

We travel around the world with "A Call for Peace Drum and Dance Company." Our performance begins with the Native American drums sounding like a heartbeat. Then we have drums from all over the world join in—from Africa, East India, the Middle East, Ireland, the Aztec people, the Hebrew people, and China. When the performance ends, it ends with that heartbeat. It's that heartbeat—that earth sound under all the many rhythms—that is the mother for all of

"I think that white Americans have to wake up and realize that the United States was multiethnic long before they came along. I think they're finally starting to see that they can't conquer what has already been here for thousands of years. . . . We might as well just get along because we're all on Mother Earth to live and survive, no matter what race, nationality, color, ethnic heritage we are."

—Art Shegonee

us and for the world. It is really getting back to the circle of respecting each other.

ART

Lots of my people ask me, "Why didn't you marry a Native American woman or someone from your own culture?" Although I was born on an Indian reservation, I was taken away and put into a foster home early on, and I grew up knowing nothing except white culture.

Some other Native Americans and I helped get rid of a local high school mascot of a Native American with a big nose, carrying a warlike hatchet.

I think that white Americans have to wake up and realize that the United States was multiethnic long before they came along. I think they're finally starting to see that they can't conquer what has already been here for thousands of years.

The way I see it, Columbus had no right taking his crosses from another country, bringing them over here, sticking them in the ground, and saying, "Well, you're all going to be Christianized whether you like it or not." And that's why we have a lot of disharmony. Our wars have been fought because of religion, not because we're different colors. One religion says to another one, "My beliefs are better than yours, so you should convert to mine." It's a disrespect of religions.

We might as well just get along because we're all on Mother Earth to live and survive, no matter what race, nationality, color, or ethnic heritage we are.

MARAL

I tell people not to do things that don't respect Indians, like go "Wa-wa-wa." My other dad is part Lakota, so I'm part Lakota. My middle name is Tate Topa. It means "four directions."

THE STEIN/KURTZ FAMILY

J. April Stein · Alan Kurtz · Rafael (6) · Julia Intia (3)

APRIL

My parents had an interfaith marriage—my dad's Jewish and my mom is a Congregationalist Yankee. I grew up in a very white, anti-Semitic community, so the Jewish part of my life was fairly hidden.

When I decided to adopt a child, I knew I didn't want to go through the process of trying to find a white baby, and I knew I really wanted to travel. Going to Peru to get Rafael and several years later to get Julia were real adventures, but I didn't really deal with the idea of adopting a child of a different race until after I got home. I didn't see the racial part. I just saw a baby.

I feel like I'm struggling with the racial issues much more now. People are starting to respond especially to Rafael as if he were Latino, which he is racially, but he isn't culturally. Who is he? And Julia is a Latina, who is also a Native American, and people think she's Korean. Who is she?

We have always exposed the kids to the music and the culture of Peru. I do want them to know and cherish their origins, but it has to be in the context of growing up in this culture.

White people are not the majority on this planet, but whites use the word "minority" in a way that keeps brown-skinned people down. I think it must have come out of a jealousy of something that's really beautiful.

When Rafael threw away all his brown crayons, we cuddled one night and talked about color. I said, "You do have a color and it's brown and that's part of who you are and I love that and it's a beautiful color."

After a school assembly on Martin Luther King Jr. Day, Rafael was confused. He looks a lot like the biracial black-white kids in his school, and he asked me if he was black. So I talked to him about race, but it was confusing to me too. What should I tell him about this? I talked about how Latinos come from different

> "I really hold to the idea of having 'children of the world' who can travel in other cultures—not just the Latino culture, but into the Native American, the Asian, and the African cultures. Children of the world!"
> —April Stein

127

parts of the world than African Americans do, although their skin colors can be the same.

Rafael is a wonderful soccer player, and many people comment that it must be because he's from Peru. Peru actually has a terrible soccer team—they are probably thinking of Brazil. I've said to them, "Do you really think there's a gene for soccer? Do you think Julia is going to be a wonderful soccer player too, because she's not showing any aptitude for sports at all?" These stereotypes are a common type of racism.

I don't understand racism. I mean I've lived with it now, but at the same time, I understand it less than ever. I really hold to the idea of having "children of the world" who can travel in other cultures—not just the Latino culture, but into the Native American, the Asian, and the African cultures. Children of the world!

ALAN

I grew up in a small, isolated, rural town that had lots of Puerto Ricans, African Americans, and Jews. I'm Jewish. My next door neighbors were Puerto Ricans, and I used to look into their apartment next door. I was fascinated by these other cultures, and I speak Spanish now partly because of that fascination back then.

The synagogue I grew up in recently had a big celebration picnic, and I noticed that Rafael was trying to take a soda. One of the women handing out food and drinks looked at him with a look that said, "This boy must have come in off the street and is trying to steal a soda." I just stood there for a moment, and then I said, "He's with me." She looked at him and looked at me. It was a very awkward moment.

I work in a clinic with many Latino clients and colleagues, and I have pictures of my children on my desk. My clients always ask, "Are these your children? Is your wife Puerto Rican?" When I tell them that my kids are adopted from Peru, they react very positively. They must feel, "He loves his children, so he must love our culture." And they're right. It's true. I do.

THE STEVENS/HARAMUT FAMILY

Penny Stevens · Matthew Haramut · Eli (9) · Matthew (6)

PENNY

My mother moved to a large university town to get her doctorate, and she liked the feeling of safety there, so we stayed. I was around more white people than black people, and I just happened to fall in love with Matt. It didn't really matter to me if he was black or white. We've been together for eleven years. Nine months ago, we separated. We're still friendly, and we co-parent the boys. The breakup had nothing to do with the color of our skin.

My mom was very supportive of my relationship with Matt. She had no problems with him being white. However, my dad was very against it. He won't even talk to our boys on the phone. Eli and Matthew don't react to that because we don't make it an issue. My mom has since remarried, and she and her husband live nearby. Now, the boys have a granddad who's the greatest granddad in the world.

Our boys are getting the best of both cultures. They know the white culture and the black culture as equals. Of course, they know about racism, and they know when people aren't treating them nicely.

I don't worry about the boys renouncing the white world. They're not followers, they're leaders.

MATTHEW

Growing up, my mom wasn't racist but my father was. For me, Penny being black didn't matter. It didn't faze me. I think the younger generations are a bit less fazed by interracial relationships. My mother was a little unsupportive at first, but then she became supportive later on. Seeing the boys played a big role in that. My dad still hasn't accepted it. He never will. Luckily, he's cordial and never rude to Penny or the boys.

"If this world is going to come together, it's inevitable that the races will mix and find harmony—and our boys are right there in the middle of that powerful group."
—Matthew Haramut

There's no outward hostility toward our family in our community. It's a sheltered area. Our boys go to a school which has so many children from diverse families that no one seems fazed by our family. They don't even notice us. Adults have to make racist remarks for the kids to put it together.

If this world is going to come together, it's inevitable that the races will mix and find harmony—and our boys are right there in the middle of that powerful group.

Penny and her mom tell the boys that they're black, but I try to explain to them that they are part black and part white. Penny says if you have any black blood at all you're considered black, which I don't agree with at all. That's what the world says, but I've explained to the boys that the world also says that black is inferior, and that isn't true either.

Right now, there's a lot of propaganda that's leading toward segregation, rather than integration. Integration is the only way. If segregation keeps happening, things are going to explode again.

THE WHEELER FAMILY

Dona Wheeler · Selin (14) · Mariah (10)

DONA

My ex-partner, Judy, and I are co-parenting the two children I adopted ten years ago. As a lesbian mom, legally I had to adopt our children as a single parent at that time. Our son arrived from El Salvador at three years old, and just eight days later his sister, a seven-week-old African American girl, completed our family.

Both Judy and I are white, yet we both felt drawn to create a multiracial family right from the beginning. I had worked with black and Hispanic families in Brooklyn and Queens for six years, but the sense of affinity—of connection—was there long before that.

Neither my father nor my sister was supportive of the adoptions—I believe they regarded them as being just one more of my typically nontraditional choices. My mother, who would have been supportive, died nine months before my children arrived. My father and my sister have both come around—in their own restrained ways—to appreciating the children. In recent years, each has expressed admiration for the quality of our family life. But it has taken time, and neither of them will ever be as nonracist as I would wish.

I thought long and hard about transracial adoption before and after I adopted my children. I've always believed that there will be a day, or a year, when one or both kids confront me or Judy angrily, demanding to know whatever possessed us to bring them into a largely white world with two moms and no dad. Or maybe it will be a subtler form of anger that doesn't lash out directly. In any event, I have rooted myself in the belief that if my two children are loved and respected for exactly who they are, they will find the internal support to withstand their having a foot in two worlds.

Once in a while, particularly when the kids were little, someone would say,

> "Each year that passes, my children become more and more of a joy. I can't imagine my life without them, and, at the same time, I love seeing them grow into their own people. Adopting them was the best decision I've ever made."
>
> —Dona Wheeler

"Oh, aren't you wonderful to do that." I think it's the other way around. Judy and I are the lucky ones.

Right now, at ten and almost fourteen, Selin and Mariah give every sign of wanting to be as much in the mainstream as possible. They are preoccupied with having as many Michael Jordan posters on their bedroom walls as possible, but I feel they will become more curious about their cultural and racial identities as they approach adulthood. We've already let them know we'll help them look for their birth parents if they decide to, and we've fantasized together about a family trip to El Salvador one day.

Child rearing has been the most challenging experience of my life so far and it has made me grow up—pushing me against my edges over and over again. Each year that passes, my children become more and more of a joy. I can't imagine my life without them, and at the same time I love seeing them grow into their own people. Adopting them was the best decision I've ever made. I like to think that our family can be a model for racial harmony and integration.

AFTERWORD: MIXED BLESSINGS

Ifeoma J. Nwokoye

"Mixed blessings." That's what my mom always used to say to try and reinforce the idea that my sisters and I were "special individuals." She wanted us to feel we had the best of two worlds as the products of an interracial marriage. She made it clear that we are not victims of our heritage or destined to live a life of anguish and confusion in a society that is so quick to judge. Rather, we should take pride in both our American and Nigerian heritages and celebrate our distinctive background. It seemed too simple a solution for such a complicated situation, yet I longed to believe her.

All humans are confronted with an identity crisis. Biracial children, too, must go through it, and for them it is a greater challenge because it's doubly hard. In our society, being both black and white is a difficult thing to deal with; you learn from the very beginning that you are supposed to be a member of some specific group and so will never be accepted for who you really are. You are born into a complex world that aims to simplify things by making divisions between races. In America, people are often unwilling to accept the idea of a biracial person. In our everyday lives we are constantly confronted with situations in which we must define who we are. We check the boxes marked *"white," "black,"* on our college forms, but there is no space marked *"multiracial"* yet. There is no place for me.

It is also twice as hard coming from two very distinct cultures—Nigerian and American. In each society I am treated in extremely different ways; yet, in both, I am identified by color. In America, I'm seen as black. I remember the time a schoolmate asked a friend of mine why she was sharing her snack with a black girl. I recall the icy stares of the ladies behind the perfume and make-up counters of every department store, their plastic smiles melting to frowns as they watched my every move. Most vividly, however, I remember how my math teacher would repeatedly confuse me with the only other black girl in the class, even until the end of the year—his belief apparently being that all black people look alike. Through all my experiences living in this culture, it has been a struggle to retain a sense of self worth.

Ironically, in Nigeria the situation is absolutely reversed. Because I am so much lighter than most people there, I am given a higher status and considered a model for others. I am treated with the utmost respect and admiration because, in their eyes, I resemble a white person. What does remain consistent in both cultures is that I am not considered a biracial person; I'm still being labeled as one or the other.

I lived in Nigeria for the first seven years of my life, and have visited on and off since my parents' divorce. As a child in Nigeria, I wasn't fully aware of people's perceptions of me, but I had a sense that I was somehow "better" than most of the children I knew, and that I had something special that they lacked. I remember being the teacher's favorite; the other students would get beaten, while I never experienced a lash of my teacher's cane. And I recall sitting in the front seat of my dad's car during a traffic jam. The little hands and noses of the village children would press hard against the window of the car, as if to penetrate the barrier of glass to steal a precious part of me. The society conditioned me to view myself as superior.

Drawing on my experience in America and in Nigeria, I have reluctantly come to the conclusion that there is no place in either of my cultures where I can be accepted for who I am. I think of the irony in both experiences, and I don't know whether to laugh or cry.

I know that I must ignore the limitations and labels society places on me, and instead, realize that I am an individual with unique insight, able to encompass the best of both worlds. I refuse to see my biracial identity as confining, and I am determined not to be defeated by other people's narrow vision. Increasingly, I am able to get strength from my inner voice and accept my own perspective on who I am. I now choose to take pride in my two cultures. I can hear my mother's soft voice, uttering those painfully simple words, letting me know that I am fortunate to have these *"mixed blessings."* And, finally, I know she is right.

RESOURCE GUIDE

BOOKS FOR ADULTS

Bartholet, Elizabeth. *Family Bonds: Adoption and the Politics of Parenting.* Boston: Houghton Mifflin Co., 1993.

Bates, J. Douglas. *Gift Children: A Story of Race, Family, and Adoption in a Divided America.* New York: Ticknor and Fields, 1993.

Brodzinksy, David, Marshall Schecter, and Robin Henig. *Being Adopted—The Lifelong Search for Self.* New York: Doubleday, 1993.

Crohn, Joel. *Mixed Matches: How to Create Successful Interracial, Inter-ethnic and Interfaith Relationships.* New York: Fawcett, 1995.

Derman-Sparks, Louise, and the A.B.C. Taskforce. *Anti-Bias Curriculum: Tools for Empowering Young Children.* Washington, DC: National Association for Child Education, 1989. Curriculum guide for proactive early childhood education plus excellent book list for children and adults.

Erlbach, Arlene. *The Families Book: True Stories about Real Kids and the People They Live With and Love.* Minneapolis, MN: Free Spirit Publishing, Inc., 1996.

Funderburg, Lise. *Black, White, Other: Biracial Americans Talk about Race and Identity.* New York: Morrow, 1994.

Haizlip, Shirlee Taylor. *The Sweeter the Juice: A Family Memoir in Black and White.* New York: Simon and Schuster Trade, 1994.

Hopson, Darlene, and Derek Hopson. *Different and Wonderful: Raising Black Children in a Race-Conscious Society.* New York: S&S Trade, Simon and Schuster, 1992.

Mathabane, Mark, and Gail Mathabane. *Love in Black and White: The Triumph of Love over Prejudice and Taboo.* New York: HarperCollins, 1993.

Mathias, Barbara, and MaryAnn French. *40 Ways to Raise a Non-Racist Child.* New York: HarperCollins, 1996.

Melina, Lois. *Raising Adopted Children.* New York: HarperCollins, 1986.

———. *Making Sense of Adoption: A Parent's Guide.* New York: HarperCollins, 1989.

Nelson-Erichsen, Jean, and Heino R. Erichsen. *Butterflies in the Wind: Spanish/Indian Children with White Parents.* Woodlands, TX: Los Ninos, 1992.

Nieto, Sonia. *Affirming Diversity: The Sociopolitical Context of Multicultural Education.* White Plains, NY: Longman, 1992.

Pohl, Constance, and Kathy Harris. *Transracial Adoption: Children and Parents Speak.* Culver City, CA: Watts, 1992.

Reddy, Maureen. *Crossing the Color Line: Race, Parenting, and Culture.* New Brunswick, NJ: Rutgers University Press, 1994.

Root, Maria P. *Racially Mixed People in America: Within, Between and Beyond Race.* Thousand Oaks, CA: Sage, 1992.

Simon, Rita J., and Howard Altstein. *Transracial Adoptees and Their Families: A Study of Identity and Commitment.* Westport, CT: Greenwood, 1987.

Tatum, Beverly. *Assimilation Blues: Black Families in a White Community.* Westport, CT: Greenwood, 1992.

Van Gulden, Holly, and Lisa Bartels-Rabb. *Real Parents, Real Children: Parenting the Adopted Child.* New York: Crossroad, 1993.

West, Cornel. *Race Matters.* Boston: Beacon Press, 1993; New York: Random House, 1994.

BOOKS FOR CHILDREN

Miller-Lachmann, Lyn. *Our Family, Our Friends, Our World: An Annotated Guide to Significant Multicultural Books for Children and Teenagers.* New Providence, NJ: R. R. Bowker, 1992. An excellent and thorough reference work that provides parents, teachers, librarians, and students with evaluations of approximately 1,000 books of fiction and nonfiction on multicultural themes.

Muse, Daphne. *The New Press Multicultural Resource Guide for Young Readers.* New York: New Press, 1997. A 700-page guide including more than 1,000 reviews of the most important multicultural children's books published from 1960 to the present. In addition, there will be a series of twenty essays, curriculum resources, and a list of book stores and libraries with outstanding multicultural literature collections.

BOOK AND RESOURCE CATALOGS FOR CHILDREN AND ADULTS

Adoptive Families of America, Inc. 2309 Como Ave., St. Paul, MN 55108. 612-535-4829, Fax: 612-535-7808. Resources on adoption and multicultural issues, including dolls, books, and tapes.

Anti-Defamation League Catalog, ADL National Headquarters, 823 U.N. Plaza, New York, NY 10017. 212-490-2525. The A WORLD OF DIFFERENCE Institute is a comprehensive, international anti-bias education and diversity training program of the ADL. The Institute's goals are to combat prejudice and discrimination of all kinds and to promote the valuing of diversity. The ADL, one of the nation's oldest human rights/human relations organizations, was founded in 1913 with two primary mandates: to stop the defamation of the Jewish people and to secure justice and fair treatment for all. ADL is one of the largest producers of human relations materials in the United States.

Chinaberry Book Catalog. 1-800-776-2242. Fax: 619-670-5203. An extraordinary annotated catalog of books and tapes for all ages of children on all topics, including multiracial, strong females, and folktales.

Everyone's Kids' Books, 23 Elliot St., Brattleboro, VT 05301. 802-254-8160. An excellent catalog of books for children and adults on gender, adoption, race, gay and lesbian issues, and culture, as well as diverse children's literature.

Great Owl Books, 41 Watchung Plaza, Suite 112, Montclair, NJ 07042. 1-800-299-3181. An excellent free catalog for children's books on multiracial/multicultural themes.

Karol Media, P.O. Box 7600, Wilkes-Barre, PA 18773-7600. 1-800-884-0555. For over twenty years, a nationwide distributor of educational and special interest videos, CD-ROM, and other resource material to the educational community. A catalog of more than 3,000 titles is available.

Lift Every Voice: Multicultural and Minority Source Materials Co., 16 Park Lane, Newton Centre, MA 02159-4775. Internet: http://www.tiac.net/users/liftever; e-mail: liftevery@aol.com. A thorough catalog of books, tapes, and videos for children and adults. More than forty cultures and fifteen languages, as well as adoption books, are listed.

The Olive Press, 5727 Dunmore, West Bloomfield, MI 48322. 810-855-6063. A catalog of multicultural books and teaching resources.

Pact Press, 3450 Sacramento, Suite 239, San Francisco, CA 94118. 415-221-6957. A catalog of 300 books for children and adults on adoption and race.

Perspectives Press, P.O. Box 90318, Indianapolis, IN 46290-0318. A publisher of many well-respected books on adoption and diversity.

Sandy & Son Educational Supplies, 1360 Cambridge St., Cambridge, MA 02139. 617-491-6290. A free catalog of wooden puzzles of interracial families.

Tapestry Books, P.O. Box 359, Ringoes, NJ 08551. 800-765-2367. e-mail: tapestry@webcom.com. A very thorough guide to books about adoption for all age levels.

Thrift Books, 9 Foxboro Circle, Madison, WI 53717. 608-833-5238. A catalog specializing in adoption and multicultural children's books, with all titles sold at 20% discount.

MAGAZINES AND NEWSLETTERS FOR TEENAGERS AND ADULTS

Adopted Child, P.O. Box 9362, Moscow, ID 83843. 208-882-1794. A monthly newsletter for parents of adopted children.

Adoptive Families Magazine, 3333 Highway 100 North, Minneapolis, MN 55422. 612-535-4829. An excellent and thorough resource for adoptive families of all kinds.

I-Pride: Interracial, Intercultural Pride, P.O. Box 11811, Berkeley, CA 94712-11811. A free newsletter published by a support group for multiracial people, which includes events, articles, and reviews.

Interrace Magazine, P.O. Box 12048, Atlanta, GA 30355. 404-355-0808. A magazine for teens and adults involved in interracial relationships. *Child of Color,* by the same publisher, is geared for parents of children five to twelve years old.

Roots and Wings Adoption Magazine, P.O. Box 577, Hackettstown, NJ 07840. 908-637-8828. A 56-page quarterly that approaches adoption from many angles.

Teaching Tolerance Magazine, Southern Poverty Law Center. 400 Washington Ave., Montgomery, AL 36104. Fax: 205-264-3121. An excellent resource provided free twice a year to educators. Schools can also send away for "The Shadow of Hate: A History of Intolerance in America," a complete teaching package available for free, including video, publication, and detailed lesson plans for teachers.

INTERNET SITES OF INTEREST

Interracial: http://www.agate.net/~wordshop/interrac.html Provides many links to interracial resources on the internet, including a state-by-state list of multiracial support groups.

Interracial Voice: http://www.webcom.com/~intvoice/ A bimonthly newsletter with updated news about political and social events nationwide. Many links to other excellent sites and home pages.

Interracial Adoption: http://www.adopting.org/inter.html. Many links to sites concerned with adoption issues.

NATIONAL INTERRACIAL SUPPORT/ADVOCACY ORGANIZATIONS

Center for the Healing of Racism, P.O. Box 27327, Houston, TX 77227.

Center for the Study of Biracial Children, c/o Francis Wardle, Ph.D., 2300 South Krameria St., Denver, CO 80222.

Harmony, P.O. Box 16996, West Palm Beach, FL 33416.

International Institute for the Healing of Racism, Route 113, Box 232, Thetford, VT 05074.

Interracial Family Circle of Washington, P.O. Box 53291, Washington, DC 20009.

I-PRIDE (Interracial Intercultural Pride), P.O. Box 11811, Berkeley, CA 94712-11811.

National Multi-Ethnic Families Association (NaMEFA), 2073 N. Oxnard Blvd, Suite 172, Oxnard, CA 93030.

Project Race (Reclassify All Children Equally, Inc.), c/o Susan Graham, 1425 Market Blvd., Suite 1320-E6, Roswell, GA 30076.

Of Many Colors: Portraits of Multiracial Families is also the title of a museum-quality, award-winning photo-text exhibit upon which this book was based. Designed to be used by people interested in bringing issues of family diversity to their communities or schools, *Of Many Colors* is available in two versions. One version of the text is age-appropriate for elementary school students (K-6), and one can be used for older students and adults.

Of Many Colors has traveled nationwide since 1994 to public and private schools (K-12), universities, houses of worship, public libraries, community centers, and museums. You can bring this exhibit to your community too.

"*Of Many Colors* was spectacular because of its comprehensive, warm and powerful depiction of families. We miss having the exhibit, and I really believe that it has already made a significant contribution to our collective understanding of each other."—Peg Scholtes, Executive Director, Family Enhancement Center, Madison, WI

For more information about bringing this exhibit to your community, please contact: Family Diversity Projects, Inc., c/o ChrisComm Management, P.O. Box 1493, Kingston, PA 18704. Phone: 717-331-3336; Fax: 717-331-3337; e-mail: chriscom@microserve.net. Visit our website at http://www.javanet.com/~FamPhoto